Testimonials

Joseph Campbell, the great mythologist, said that religions need to change with time in order to remain relevant in people's lives, and that religions that do not change die. Sam Alexander realizes this. He is performing CPR on traditional Christianity, helping it evolve in order to remain a vivifying force in the modern world. For those who feel the tug of the transcendent through Christ's teachings, Evolving Christianity *can be a magnificent, life-changing experience.*

Larry Dossey, MD
Author of One Mind: How Our Individual Mind Is Part of a Greater Consciousness and Why It Matters

I don't listen to many Christian teachers because it is rare to hear one whose voice resonates so clearly with the love radiating from within the foundations of creation. Too often the teachings are exclusionary and judgmental, but that is not what we get from Sam Alexander. Instead the way he describes his faith, invites people to engage Christ's teachings in a way that is intelligible in our world and faithful to his own, while bringing the reader, whether she agrees with him or not, into a conversation that opens all of us to new possibilities. In his hands, Christian faith is a viable, electric path into the presence of Spirit. Finally, I have a way to talk to my Christian friends!

Mariana Caplan, PhD, MFT, psychotherapist, yoga teacher, consultant, and the author of seven books including the forthcoming: *Yoga & Psyche* (Sounds True, 2015) and *Eyes Wide Open: Cultivating Discernment on the Spiritual Path* (Sounds True, 2009)

Every Christian, every person who is driven to find meaning, who passionately seeks harmony, or who is deeply troubled by inherent contradiction, should know something about Evolutionary Christianity and there is no one better to learn it from than Sam Alexander. Nobody tussles with Christian dogma quite like he does. His honest soul-searching, lively arguments and sparkling stories may do more than change your mind. They may just change your life.

Rev. Jana L. Childers, Ph.D.
Dean, San Francisco Theological Seminary, author and editor of numerous books and articles including, P*erforming the Word, and Birthing the Sermon.*

Sam Alexander's work offers us a thoughtful, balanced, and heart-saturated approach to spirit for our time. Highly recommended.

Sally Kempton
author of *Meditation for the Love of It and Awakening Shakti*

Sam allows us to feel his love for the sacred texts, his struggle with modernity and postmodernity and his heroic reaching towards an authentic synthesis . . . most central, however, is the understated depth of his insight which has the fragrance of wisdom.

Marc Gafni, D.Phil.,
author of ten books, including the national bestseller *Soul Prints, and The Mystery of Love*. Gafni is the founder of Unique Self theory. His most recent book is *Your Unique Self: The Radical Path to Personal Enlightenment*

Christianity began as a pluralistic faith response to experiences of overwhelming Divine love and grace, but somewhere along the way too many of us have lost sight of that. We don't have to agree on every detail to be in love with God and to love what God loves. The book that my friend and col-

league, Sam Alexander, has written is a brilliant reconstructive move to return our postmodern attention to the awesome faith of our spiritual grandmothers and grandfathers—the faith that experiences the living God—the God calling to us all from the future, and who is present right here, right now. Sam's book deserves to be read by a wide audience that may or may not agree with him, but who hope to find access to a useful and fascinating platform for participating in the on-going in-breaking of God's light and love into a world starving for spiritual nourishment."

Fr. John Forman OblSB, MDiv
Rector, St. Elizabeth Episcopal Church,
Burien, Washington, and author of
"Integral Leadership: The Next Half-Step"

Evolving Christianity;
Life After Faith Crisis

by Rev. Samuel G. Alexander

© Copyright 2015 by Rev. Samuel G. Alexander

All rights reserved. No part of this book may be reproduced without written permission from Rev. Samuel G. Alexander, 238 Ridgeway Ave., Fairfax, CA 94930

Bible quotations, unless otherwise noted, are from the *New Revised Standard Version*, copyright 1989, Division of Christian Education of the National Council of the Churches of Christ in the United States of America. Used by permission. All rights reserved.

Evolving Christianity; Life After Faith Crisis
by Rev. Samuel G. Alexander

ISBN: 978-0-9963418-0-6

To Barbara Alexander

without whom I would never have known the power of God's love.

Table of Contents

Foreword by Marc Gafni vii

Preface xv

Introduction xxi
    Who Should Read This Book and Who Shouldn't xxi
    What Do I Mean by Evolutionary Christianity? xxiii
    Sources for a Conversation.. xxix
    The Structure of the Book xxxi

PART I: UNIQUE SELF AS SEEN THROUGH THE CHRISTIAN SCRIPTURES 1
    Chapter 1: Power to Become Children of God 5
    Chapter 2: We Are in This Together 17
    Chapter 3: Ethical Imperative 31
    Chapter 4: Stress Drives Evolution 37
    Chapter 5: Progress of Meaning 47

PART II: THEOLOGICAL QUESTIONS FOR EVOLUTIONARY CHRISTIANS 57
    Chapter 6: Why Preach on the Bible in the Twenty-First Century? 59
    Chapter 7: Making Sense of the Cross? 66
    Chapter 8: Trinity and the Three Faces of Spirit 73
    Chapter 9: The Trouble with Sin 87
    Chapter 10: Does Prayer Work? 97

PART III: SO WHAT DOES THIS DEMAND OF US? 106
    Chapter 11: Wake Up, Grow Up, Show Up 108
    Chapter 12: Meet Me in Galilee 118

PART IV: APPENDICES 125
    Two Spiritual Exercises You Might Have Missed 126
    Death of the Church 134
    Continuing the Conversation 140
    Afterword by Barbara Alexander 142

Foreword by Marc Gafni

Sam Alexander has written a very important book. In it he outlines a vision of evolutionary Christianity, which is vital for the next stage of Christian emergence. His voice is insightful, humble, and powerful all at the same time. He allows us to feel his love for the sacred texts, his struggle with modernity and postmodernity and his heroic reaching towards an authentic synthesis. In reading I was delighted by Sam's voice, his style, and his honesty, but most of all by the depth of his insight, which has the fragrance of wisdom. The emergence of the next level of consciousness in Christianity needs Sam Alexander. I loved this little book and am hoping to be hearing more from its author in future.

In this introduction I want to locate Sam's work and its significance in the larger framework of a world spirituality. I will first try and articulate what Ken Wilber and I mean when we talk about World Spirituality and then identify Sam's work as a *primary expression of "dual citizen" Christianity,* within that larger context.

An Emergent World Spirituality

Every human being yearns to understand the patterns that connect everything and that reveal a glimmer of the intention and purpose of existence. Transmitting a vision of the patterns that connect used to be the province of the great religious traditions. This is often called the pre-modern or the traditional worldview. The religions have profound wisdom about the true nature of the human being. They provided a compelling vision of the good life, what a life well lived looked like. Yet the religions overplayed their hand in a number of ways. First, they claimed more certainty then they had. The church, for example, claimed to know that the earth was flat, that the planets revolved around the earth, how many bones were in a human body. When empirical scientific information disproved these claims we began to lose our trust in the church.

Second, as consciousness evolved and we began to realize that all human beings are equal and endowed with infinite worth and dignity, democracy and universal human rights became cornerstones of Western enlightenment. In light of these advances, different religions' claims of their intrinsic superiority seemed ridiculous. Trust in the church was further undermined.

It is for this very good reason that a new worldview, that of modernity, displaced the traditional or pre-modern worldview. Modernity attempted to erect a temple of reason in which it would be able to reconstruct a new secular vision of the good life. This vision affirmed human dignity, choice, and capacity. The grand narrative of modernity, the modernist vision, was filled with implicit assumptions about the goodness of life, moral obligation, and about the personal obligation to engage in self-development and self-transformation. This new worldview produced the great movements of psychology, evolutionary theory, human rights, democracy, and free markets based not on authentic certainty but on reason. Modernity demolished the certainties of the church. In its place emerged the certainties of science coupled with a kind of stylish uncertainty about virtually all ultimate issues of meaning and value.

Postmodernity came along and rejected the grand narrative of both pre-modernity (the traditional religious worldview) and modernity (the rational worldview of western science). Postmodernity pointed out the implicit spiritual assumptions in modern values and used those assumptions to discredit modernity's truth claims. Postmodernity took over the western universities and became highly popular in culture. Its basic position was that the only grand narrative of meaning is that there is no grand narrative. You cannot look for the patterns that connect because they do not connect. This position claims that there are no universals, there is no ultimate meaning beyond what was called "the merely subjective." We are left then with what can be drawn from different merely subjective fields, to create a shared world philosophy, since there is no underlying set of shared truths that can address ultimate issues of meaning, purpose, and value.

As Rev. Alexander will show in this book, the postmodern grand narrative turns out not to be true either. In fact it turns out that a careful study of all the great disciplines reveals a truly powerful grand narrative of meaning. This narrative is not static but evolving. Indeed evolution itself is a core part of the narrative. This narrative is drawn from every field of human inquiry including science, mysticism, psychology, medicine, economics, physics, history, and the key shared insights of all the great traditions. For the first time in history we are able to articulate an integral vision of meaning that can potentially create a shared language of meaning – one that honors diversity even as it sees a compelling vision of meaning and value, a vision that unites us far more deeply than anything that divides us. An articulation of this vision is emerging from a kind of Manhattan Project taking place at the Center for Integral Wisdom, and particularly in our World Spirituality project, a project in which Rev. Alexander is intimately involved. In this great project we are studying and extracting the core strands of agreed upon meaning from all of the world's wisdom sources. We are then linking them together into a grand narrative of meaning, one which bows before the mystery even as it has the power to inspire a values-driven, purpose-driven life.

We believe that the cogent articulation of a World Spirituality is the critical challenge of our time. The articulation of such a World Spirituality, articulated in a language that mainstream culture can understand, one that has the power to penetrate culture, is both the urgent necessity and the great invitation of our time. It may well be the most important next move we can make in the evolution of consciousness.

To be clear, a world spirituality is not a religion. It is not a science. It is neither, yet both. World Spirituality transcends yet includes the best of religion and science. Like a great religion it offers guidance in every sphere of life. Like science it is fact based not only faith based. It is what in Sanskrit is called Dharma. It is not dogma. Dharma – a term we will engage during the book - implies a deep personal certainty of knowing that each of us can access directly, not a mere cultural belief imposed upon us. You cannot know dogma directly; rather it is imposed on you from outside. You are required to believe it by a religious institution or by a society, even though you cannot validate its truth with your experience. Nevertheless you are required to believe the dogma if you are to achieve some version of salvation, or redemption, or inclusion into the community. *World Spirituality is a dharma not a dogma.*

Why a World Spirituality?

Every human being lives in an inescapable framework. That framework – which has also been called a worldview—is sometimes conscious but more often then not it is unconscious. Your worldview is the colored glasses through which you see reality. Your worldview is not extra; it is everything. It is what allows you to make meaning. It the hidden decider that guides every key life decision you make. It determines how you spend your time and how you spend your money.

Most people in the world fall into one of the three worldviews we've described. Seventy percent of the world lives their life guided by the dogma of a particular religion or belief system that significantly invalidates the people outside of that religion. The smaller slice of the world pie does not believe we can know anything objective or real about spirit, or meaning, or the ultimate meaning of reality. This slice of the world believes that only objective science or data driven facts are true. Everything else is up to personal preference, which is rooted in subjective cultural mores. This is a combination of the modern and the postmodern worldview. Each one of these belief systems is a framework or worldview within which we live our lives, make decisions, and find meaning.

There is, however, a fourth worldview, what Sam and I call an Integral world spirituality framework. This integral framework is drawn together from the best of every source of wisdom. It is fully accessible to the common person. Moreover it is truly stunning in its life empowering and transformative impact on every single person who realizes it. This integral framework addresses every dimension of human life in ways that are startlingly original, fresh, and compelling. Included are all the major questions in regard to issues of love, sexuality, relationships as well as meaning values and purpose.

This is a framework of dharma not dogma. Dharma says that every system of meaning in the world, every philosophy, every psychology and every religion is *true but partial*. Therefore there is room for everyone at the table.

Take for example what I like to call the "Story of Two Ricks." One, Richard Dawkins, the author of the cult classic, *The Selfish Gene*, is an evolutionary theorist who is a self-avowed atheist. He is antagonistic about anything to do with spirit or the ultimate, inviolable, purpose and meaning. The second, Rick Warren, author of *The Purpose Driven Life,* is an evangelical Christian. A genuine World Philosophy dharma integrates the position of each Rick by affirming that both are speaking an important part of the story. Each Rick's position is true but partial. Weaving them together we get a deeper truth that has never been available before at any previous time in history.

This new world spirituality addresses, in different ways, all the worldviews we've discussed above. It provides a structure for what dual citizenship. A dual citizen lives within and is committed to a great religious tradition without believing that tradition is exclusively right, therefore being both a member of a religious tradition and a global citizen who shares a vision of meaning and spirit with the rest of the world. This group can be enormously influential in shaping the future. *This group draws on the power of the lineages from within while audaciously engaging in their evolution, not as critics but as lovers. Rev. Alexander and his work are prime exemplars of this great tradition. There is no higher compliment that I could give his work.*

Others who engage a World Spirituality are post traditional. The post traditionalist rejects the old religions but embraces an eclectic spirituality. A shared world spirituality is obviously necessary for both the dual citizen and the post traditional global citizen. However it is also relevant for the traditionalist, the modernist, and the postmodernist. Often the reason a person embraces a fundamentalist worldview is not because they believe the dogma. Rather, they embrace it because they view a fundamentalist community as being committed, rooted in a moral context, and driven by values and purpose. By contrast more liberal, modern or postmodern communities seem tepid, uncommitted, and without deeply rooted values or commitments. A world wisdom philosophy that is able to formulate a vision of commitment, ethics, passion, and responsibility would challenge the fundamentalist assumption that these key qualities are only available in a fundamentalist worldview. Finally a world philosophy that validates the authority of science and powerfully embraces the critical values of modernity would be a spiritual wisdom that even the secularist can find compelling.

Grounded in the Christian tradition, this book will present no less then a new story of meaning – a new Universe Story – which has the power to become the cornerstone of joy, meaning, and purpose for the new millennium. In that sense it is a contrarian book. It cannot be labeled either liberal or neoconservative. It is neither secular nor religious. It is neither exclusively scientific nor spiritual. Rather, it weaves a larger framework of meaning that includes them all in the most simple and clear terms. This is the simplicity after complexity and not before complexity. It takes into account all of the complexity and then seeks the underlying guiding principles which form a compelling, potent, non-dogmatic vision of the patterns that connect.

We Need This Now

1. For the first time in history, the core challenges to survival we face today are not local to a particular religion, country, or region. They are world challenges, ranging from the very real threats to the ground we walk on and the air we breathe, to world hunger, to the danger of nuclear weapons falling into the hands of a rogue state, to the most pressing issues of social and economic justice. There is no place left to hide, and the spiritual truth of the interconnectedness of all things is no longer a hidden teaching but an obvious truth. Whenever new life conditions come to pass, an evolutionary leap in consciousness and culture is required to meet them. The global challenges we face require the evolution of a new spiritual consciousness in which we realize that what unites us is so much greater then what divides us: we need a World Spirituality.

2. For the first time in history we can all talk to each other. More than that: for the first time in history we must all talk to each other. For anyone even vaguely awake as a World Citizen, there is a dawning realization that we can only solve the radical challenges of our time through collective action. Collective action requires a shared framework of meaning. Shared meaning motivates shared action.

3. For the first time in history, there is a critical mass of at least two hundred million people who have reached this world-centric consciousness. These people have expanded their circle of caring and concern beyond their ethnocentric affiliations. They are at home in the world and feel responsible

for the world as a whole, and not merely for their country or religion.

4. For the first time in history, the most profound teachings as well as living teachers from all the great systems of spirit are readily available in a non-coercive and open-hearted form, not only to people of their particular religion, but to all who wish to come to study and practice with them.

5. For the first time in history, the notion of dual citizenship is readily understood and available. Not only can one be a citizen of two countries, but one can also remain committed to one's native or chosen spiritual tradition, while at the same time being a citizen of World Spirituality.

6. For the first time in history, there are hundreds of millions of well-educated people who, although they cannot find their homes in the traditional religions, are searching for a compelling universal set of meaning principles by which they can live their lives.

This book provides an interpretation of Christianity that is informed by dual citizenship in a world spirituality and contributes to that world spirituality. Christian or not, agree with him or not, I hope you enjoy it as I have.

Marc Gafni, D.Phil., Pacific Grove, January 2014

Preface

Once upon a time I was an evangelical Christian. But now, having pastored a mainline Protestant church, I find myself musing that I need a little help over here on the dark side. Evangelical faith has three qualities that are in short supply and desperately needed in the "progressive" wing of the church. First, evangelicals believe that the Bible has authority in their lives. I believe that. (My Liberal colleagues don't quite know what to make of my unreasonable attachment to the Scriptures.) Second, they believe that Christian faith is about transformation. I believe that too. Third, they think it is important to share their faith with other people. Wow, do I believe that! But I worry that we've watered down the message of Christian hope so far that the mainline Church is finding its meaning or direction in something like the phrase, "Jesus was nice, so we should be nice too." Perhaps more disturbing is that we seem to be living under the dictum "live as long as you can just as comfortably as you can," as though that's all there is to this life. There is a reason for this. That's why I'm writing this book.

At its best, evangelical faith is alive, it feeds the soul, and it provides a context of meaning for those who can believe. I say "can believe" because in a modern world, a world where we have snapped pictures of distant galaxy fields and our own DNA, believing in a traditional God, the one who can be called upon to fix things with the snap of His fingers when they've gone terribly wrong, is becoming more and more problematic. Frankly, a lot of the time it feels like we're stretching the limits of credulity.

How did we get here? The trouble starts, and this may sound a little strange, when we send our children to school. When they go to school they learn about everything from quarks to evolution. Then we take them back to church where they're told that God is the one who is doing the creating, but we never quite get around to explaining how those two ideas can co-exist. What we learn in school and what we learn in any self-respecting Evangelical church derives from mutually exclusive worldviews. It's a real problem, a real disconnect.

In the mainline church the problem is a little different, but it's huge. I think it is why the mainline church is dying. Many solid mainline congregations use traditional mythic language. We sing the old hymns and say some of the old creeds and prayers, (though less and less these days). We say them, but oftentimes, maybe even most of the time, we don't believe them. So why do we bother? My cousin Richard says, "It's kind of like a secret handshake. If we just say the words then we get to be part of this cool club, we get to hang out with some nice people doing some good things in the world." For the most part, mainline Christians don't believe anything that runs directly counter to a modernist worldview; we've pretty well deconstructed traditional Christianity, but we've also failed to reconstruct anything compelling in its place. Ask people why they go to a mainline church and the answer you usually get is, "I go for the community." Society is changing. People can find community in many other places these days, so with not much more than a deconstructed faith to offer, people have left the mainline church in droves. They leave because the language we insist on using – whether we believe it or not – doesn't make sense to the modern mind.

Consider: we Christians say that God has a son who was executed on a cross approximately 2000 years ago, that his blood was shed for us, and as a result, (if we believe it), you and I, two thousand years later, get to go to heaven instead of that other place. Now I should probably make myself clear here lest you write me off as a "non-believer." Truth be told, I *am* a believer. Believe it or not, there is some sense in which I do trust that "Jesus died for my sins" . . . but the real question is, "What do I mean when I say it?" (I try to answer that one in Chapter 7.)

Two thousand years ago people thought blood had magical properties, that it could affect their relationship to the creator. But we don't think that anymore so what could it possibly mean to say that Jesus died for our sins? This is the moment when a traditionalist says something like, "It's a mystery. We cannot fathom the ways of God, so we must simply trust that God's word is true, that God's promises are reliable, that God is love," and leave it at that.

Then, when someone is sick, or needs a job, or is struggling to remain faithful in his marriage, we pray for that God to intervene. But let's face it: counting on a miraculous intervention is a little dicey. Interventions seem to happen some of the time, but seldom enough to give us pause. So again we end up looking for ways to let God off the hook for unanswered prayer. For instance, a line of "comfort" offered to my wife, at the time a grieving nine year-old was, "Barbara, I know it's hard to understand, but God needs your daddy more than you do right now."

Or we pray for events beyond ourselves, for world peace, or an end to suffering; we ask how a loving God allows millions of children to die each year. But war keeps on going (43 of them at the moment), and children still die even though we have the resources to keep them alive – the resources, but apparently not the will. We let God off the hook for this too; we say human sin is the problem. We are the ones that perpetrate the horror; God can't do anything about it without taking away our free will. I don't buy it. This is God we're talking about. Can't God find a way to eliminate human suffering without violating human freedom? Granted, I can't figure out how to do it, but we're theoretically talking about God the almighty, eternal, infinite, creator of all that is. Why should that be a stretch? So we reaffirm to ourselves, "God has a plan, God is just, God is loving; trust in the Lord, He is worthy."

But each time that this interventionist, magic God lets us down, each time that we need to come up with another excuse for God's action or inaction, our faith strains. Eventually the only thing that props it up is gathering with other believers and repeating over and over phrases like "Jesus died for our sins," "God in three persons, blessed Trinity," "God answers prayer," or "He is worthy." We repeat the words as if willing them to be true, as if demanding they make sense of the life we are actually living.

Eventually I couldn't do that anymore. I couldn't make excuses for God any more. It happened when my wife died many years ago after a long, long, illness. We had prayed and prayed; she died in shame, when our kids were still young, thinking that there was something fundamentally wrong with her, something that made her unlovable; she died thinking that her death was God's judgment on her life. In the end I realized that one of two things was true: either the God I'd been talking about lo those many years does not exist, or God hates me and so had decided to punish me through my wife's death. My early faith began to unravel.

Tolstoy describes a dream in his little book, *Confessions*. It speaks to my unraveling faith. He was lying on a rope mattress when he noticed that one of the ropes had come unraveled. He didn't think much of it, but then another came loose . . . and another . . . and another, until he began to worry: what was underneath the bed? He looked over the edge and found that it was suspended over a deep, dark, terrifying abyss. Then more and more ropes came unraveled until he was left balancing on one last rope. He looked to see where the rope was attached and saw that it was tied very securely to a massive white pillar. But the pillar too was suspended over the abyss!

Just like in Tolstoy's dream, the faith to which I had clung for so long unraveled before my eyes. There were no ropes and no bed to hold me up, so I did what people do when the underpinnings of their traditional faith lie in tatters on the ground: I became a liberal, God forbid. I entered the vast spiritual wasteland, the deep dark abyss I'd avoided for so long.

But I have moved from that place for I have come to know that:

by and by the gale dies down and the moon rises and throws a lane of gold to us across the blackness and heaving of the tumbling waters. After all it is not in the day, but in the night that star rises after star, and constellation follows constellation, and the immensity of this bewildering universe looms up before our staggered mind. And it is in the dark that the faith becomes biggest and bravest, that its wonder grows yet more and more.[1]

Fresh faith, fresh light does emerge and I've found that when that light emerges it becomes brighter and brighter until you look into the abyss and know with certainty that you could fall forever and never escape the loving arms of God. That's the faith I want to share.

The idea that a God who created the universe 13.82[2] billion years ago, a universe so large it defies comprehension, the idea that God needs the shedding of blood to satisfy His sense of justice is to me, unbelievable. To think that there is a God somewhere out there who intervenes to rescue some from calamity but leaves others to suffer, runs so counter to John's view that "God is love,"[3] at least to me is ludicrous. The trouble is that if you've grown up with an evangelical faith you feel as if you HAVE to believe it. It feels as if life depends on you believing it. At least it felt that way to me. Leaving that early faith and entering the vast spiritual wasteland of modernism seemed unthinkable. I was a pastor, for crying out loud. That is how I felt.

But I have learned it is not so.

Not everyone has taken such an intense journey. But there are plenty of people who know the myth cannot stand,

---

1. Arthur Gossip, "When Life Tumbles in, Then What?" (Sermon preached shortly after his wife had died.)
2. They keep changing this number on us! 13.82 is the latest estimate based I'm told, on measurements of background radiation in the cosmos.
3. John 4:8.

that a magic God in the heavens doesn't make sense of the facts. I see people who have deconstructed traditional faith and are left wanting. Now if you've found a faith that sustains you and moves you towards transformation, I have no need or desire to change your path. I am writing for those who haven't and who long for something real in the midst of the struggle of life, for those who have noticed the ropes coming unraveled, those who feel stuck in a vast spiritual wasteland.

This book begins my effort to describe the faith I've found in the abyss. I believe it is gospel—good news. It is a Christian faith to be sure, for as I look at the Christian scriptures I understand the authors to be pointing towards truth in the only way they could, from within their own worldview. My desire and commitment is to be faithful to those texts, pointing at the same truth from within mine. I want to shed light on the abyss, to offer individuals another way to understand Christian faith, to offer a context of meaning.

I write this book to say one thing: We need not fear the vast spiritual wasteland because there is a rich landscape of spiritual life on the other side. There are other ways of describing the good news of God's creative power and love, the creative love of God expressed in Jesus Christ. Belief in an interventionist God is not required in order to lay hold of a rich, transformative, Christian faith, a faith that requires no excuses, is faithful to the Scriptures, proclaims a God of grace transforming all our lives, and is most certainly a gospel worth sharing.

Introduction

Who Should Read This Book and Who Shouldn't

This is a book about faith development in the Christian tradition. I know that the Church has a bad name. Frankly we deserve it. Century after century we have taken a profound message of hope, one founded on the creative, loving nature of God, and perverted it. From Emperor Constantine to Hitler we have allied ourselves with those who distort Christ's message in an effort to inspire fear. We have created categories of "us" and "them," dividing rather than joining people together in perfect harmony.[4] With great regularity we have taken a stunning message of transformation and turned it into moralistic pablum devoid of the power needed to drive us toward development and growth. Like I said, the church has a bad name and we deserve it.

Yet even having said that, I believe the Christian message offers profound hope for the future development of the world. It is that hope I want to share. What I write is not intended for everybody, so let me first describe those people I specifically do not want to engage.

If while reading this book you find yourself getting angry with what I say, if you think I'm heretical, if you think it is odd that I have not yet been struck dead by the Almighty, you can be pretty sure I am not writing this book for you, so please stop reading. I have enough respect for your point of view that I don't need to change it. Or, if you jettisoned the

---

4. Above all, clothe yourselves with love, which binds everything together in perfect harmony. And let the peace of Christ rule in your hearts, to which indeed you were called in the one body" (Colossians 3:14-15).

whole religion thing a while ago and have instead developed a spiritual practice that lights up your inner life and draws you towards an ever more beautiful tomorrow, this book isn't necessarily written for you either. Dr. Gafni did however refer to the "gentle voice" I've used in writing it, so maybe it wouldn't hurt to read what I've written.

I am not writing to those who are relatively stable in their faith development. I'm writing for those who are restless, who know on the inside that something needs to shift. I do not believe that everyone needs to shift; I do not believe that the Christian message is the only message of hope or that it is the best one for everyone. I am, as Dr. Gafni described, a "dual citizen." I am clearly Christian but recognize the value of engaging other faith perspectives as all of us seek to grow in union with the God we are all coming to know.

But see if something like this sounds familiar: I always believed that God was up there watching over me. I always believed that if I prayed God would hear my prayer. He might not always answer my prayer, but that is because God knows best. I was taught that I am a sinner, deserving of damnation, and were it not for the fact that God's son, Jesus Christ, died on the cross for me, well then damned I would be. But I'm having difficulty making sense of that anymore. If there is such a God, then why does that God allow suffering to exist? Why does He allow my suffering to exist? I can't reconcile that God with what I know about the way our world works, but I am nervous, maybe even scared, to let go of my faith.

If that sounds familiar to you, then please read this book. The Christian message does not have to be understood in those mythic terms. The God you no longer believe in doesn't exist. Never did. You don't have to let go of your faith. It can be a difficult and challenging project to develop a new understanding of faith, but it is enriching; it is life changing.

Or maybe something like this sounds familiar: I left the idea of a magic God in the dust a long time ago. Church long ago stopped making sense to me. The idea that a loving God allows suffering to exist, or that entire groups of people are consigned to a place of suffering for all eternity just because they grew up in a culture that didn't believe in Jesus is simply absurd. The church makes its moralizing pronouncements, but let's face it, its morals leave a great deal to be desired. Church is not for me. I've been calling myself spiritual but not religious of late. I've tried out several things over the years; some have been helpful, but right now it just feels to me as if there's something missing and I've started to wonder whether beneath all that I've abhorred about the church there might be something that can help me take a step forward in my life, something that can offer me a clearer view of purpose and a deeper way of contending with the realities of a world in outrageous pain.

Please, please read this book. I make no claim to have all the answers, but I believe the tradition of your youth has something profound to offer a world in outrageous pain and that there is a God of outrageous, creative love. In both of these cases, whether you long ago walked away from Christian faith or are just now beginning to struggle with the traditional language of the faith, I believe what is happening in you is an evolution of consciousness, a movement from one religious worldview to another, to another. Your understanding and your relationship to Christian faith is evolving and that is a wonderful thing indeed!

What Do I Mean by Evolutionary Christianity?

This book seeks to explore Christian faith from the point of view of its evolution, for Christianity, like everything else in the universe, evolves. The following chapters speak of the impact this has on our lives but are not theoretical in nature, so I thought it would be good to explain just a bit of the framework I use when interpreting my tradition.

For years, theorists have charted these evolutionary

moves from one religious worldview to another to another.[5] Everything evolves. Developmental theorists have not only charted a spiritual line of development, they have charted the physical line of development, (two year olds to ninety year olds), the evolutionary line that developed our species, (homo erectus or before to homo sapiens), the technical line of development, (hunter-gatherer to information technology), a moral line of development, and so on. Everything evolves.[6]

Morally human beings evolve from being egocentric, caring only about the self and those that serve us, (think two-year-old), to ethnocentric, caring for the group of which we are a part, (our particular community, whether local, political, religious, a sports team or whatever), to worldcentric, caring for all people in the world, (think Jimmy Carter), to kosmocentric[7], caring for all sentient beings, (think Al Gore). Here is what's important: as we evolve along any line of development, each stage transcends and includes the stage before it, (or at least we hope it does). So, we don't stop caring for our family when we start caring for all the people in the world.

Everything evolves. We evolve individually and our groupings evolve. And we don't just evolve externally; individuals and groups evolve internally as well. And, each line of development has an impact on other lines of development. For instance, we were not able to develop technologically beyond being hunter-gatherers until our physical brains had evolved, and we could not evolve culturally until an agricultural technology made it advantageous for us to settle in cities. Creation is an extraordinarily complex weave of individual and group evolution, both internal and external. Everything evolves and

---

5. See, for instance, James Fowler's work in *Stages of Faith: the Psychology of Human Development and the Quest for Meaning*.
6. I would point the reader to the extraordinary body of work by Ken Wilber, listed in the bibliography, to more fully understand the far-reaching implications of this one little statement.
7. Kosmocentric, a term coined by Ken Wilber, refers to the Pythagorean term "Kosmos" meaning the pattern or order that connects the universe throughout its many dimensions of physical, mental, and spiritual existence.

it evolves through stages.

And so does our religion or spirituality. Once upon a time nomad tribes related by blood walked the earth and for the most part it appears they envisioned a world populated by spirits. They interacted and connected to the Divine[8] through magic (think coconuts and pineapples offered to an active volcano). But at some point, when we developed agricultural technology and settled in cities, larger groups had to come together to protect their interests. The ones who didn't were pushed out of the gene pool; they're not with us anymore. This is how nations developed. Blood could no longer be the bond holding such a large group together and so for that and other reasons, human beings developed religions. Those religions gave the group identity; the religious narratives also gave the group an understanding of their purpose in creation and a framework to understand the connections they were making to the Divine.

So, for instance, over time a group of tribes came together in what is now Israel and developed a narrative about the sons of Jacob who had the same name as the tribes that were banding together into a nation. They experienced and understood God through these narratives. Other groups of tribes, other nascent nations had other narrative ways of forming larger community.

Over time nations interacted with other nations. Some were defeated and subsumed into the conquering nation. As that process happened the narratives shifted and changed. Some disappeared, some experienced resurgence as they reinvented themselves. Religions are like languages: they are part and parcel of cultural evolution which is in turn influenced by technological evolution, physical evolution, and so on. For

---

8. This being a book on faith development, I am making the fundamental faith assumption that there is a Divine something to connect to, however we might describe it. I grant that this cannot be rationally proven, though I think there is enough evidence to suggest that such faith is not irrational. I mean really, 13.82 billion years from the Big Bang to Shakespeare tells me that positing the existence of a "something," that in its most general form I name "the Divine," is rational.

millennia these narratives evolved, the stories were told to construct meaning to offer a purpose in the world, and the laws and expectations drawn from the stories inspired connection to God and offered a path of transformation.

Christianity itself emerged when the Hebrew narrative met and was profoundly influenced by the Greco-Roman narrative. Protestant Christianity evolved and changed in part because of political considerations in Europe. Everything evolves, and evolution along one line of development impacts evolution along other lines of development.

Then something big happened. The traditional-mythic religions of the world met modernism. They still haven't recovered. Modernism is characterized by the search for truth through scientific observation and experimentation. Modernism had a huge creative impact on our technological development, our political development, and so on. But modernism deconstructed the traditional-mythic narratives that had given us our purpose and had offered a path of transformation. Whenever the modernist worldview becomes dominant in human culture it seems that the religious-spiritual line of development atrophies. There is simply no place for a mythic God in a modernist worldview. No wonder the churches started to empty. What's the point?

Well of course there is a point. We still need a sense of purpose. We still need a framework in which to develop and grow in relation to the Divine. So if the idea of simply deconstructing the traditional narratives, narratives which have given human beings purpose and connection to the Divine for so long, and doing so without reconstructing something in their place – if that seems like a questionable project to you, then I'm with you. Sticking our collective head in the sand and pretending that modernism will go away doesn't strike me as a productive strategy for the church either. We simply must reconstruct meaning and connection to the Divine if humanity is to develop and grow. Living without any sense of purpose beyond "he who has the most toys when he dies wins" is not a pretty picture.

Of course many people have awoken to that fact. It is no accident that the "Spirituality" section at your local bookstore, (assuming you still have a local bookstore), is so big. This is a great thing! Postmodern consciousness has come online. We have come to recognize that there are innumerable perspectives, and that no one of them can make an exclusive claim to the truth. So wherever modernism takes hold people leave their churches in droves, our religious line of development atrophies, but now as postmodernism takes hold, we seek meaning and connection to the Divine in other places. Alleluia, I say! Spirit is alive and well even if the church is not.

But what's interesting to me is that very often we leave the religious structure of our youth (in my culture that is usually some form of Christianity) and seek that meaning and connection in a different traditional-mythic narrative, often of an Eastern religion that emphasizes practice, not narrative. If you feel as if you have found such a vibrant practice and been able to integrate it into your life, I think that's wonderful. Go in peace! But I've found that many people sense a kind of prompting to make peace with or rediscover the theological language of their youth from a more evolved stage of consciousness. For more than a decade I've been working to put into practice a life that plumbs the depths of Christian faith from a place that transcends the mythic frame and embraces Christianity's mystical past.

Many people have come to call this the Integral stage in the evolution of consciousness. It is the foundation for the "dual-citizenship" model of world spirituality that Marc Gafni talked about in the Foreword to this book. We have transcended the mythic stage of consciousness by accepting the insights of modernism and deconstructing the myth, but we include it as we recognize that our mythic forbears had a valid experience of the Divine that they described through the myth. I seek to understand what the authors of the Bible were pointing at, rather than believing what they say is literally true.

This is another way of saying what Marc referred to in

the Foreword: as I interpret biblical texts I am seeking to get at dharma, the spiritual life inherent in the texts, a life that can be validated by human experience. These are truths we can come to know as we seek, rather than statements of supposed fact imposed upon the seeker.

The authors of the biblical texts were writing out of experiences they had with God, but they were describing them from within their own worldview, not ours. The dharma question asks, "What experience of God was the author of the Gospel of John pointing toward when he wrote, "For God so loved the world that he gave His only begotten Son that whosoever believes in Him shall not perish but have everlasting life?"[9] Why did he put it that way? A dogmatic interpretation on the other hand says, "Jesus died for your sins. If you want to be saved you have to believe that."

We also seek to transcend the postmodern, pluralistic stage by recognizing the value of being grounded in a particular tradition, but we very much want to include a postmodern perspective by realizing we have no claim to exclusive truth. From that stance, grounded in a tradition, but not claiming an exclusive grasp on its truth, we can engage in constructive conversation with those who are doing the very same thing from within other religious traditions.[10] In fact these are the conversations that I've found most enriching. They have challenged me to become a deeper and more committed Christian.

I am writing to help people who are deconstructing their traditional faith. I'm writing for people who question the validity of a magical God and yet have misgivings about letting go of faith. I'm also writing for people who deconstructed the myth some time ago but find that a full and complete reconstruction evades them. For ten years I've traveled that

---

9. John 3:16.
10. There is a growing group of people who are seeking a religious structure that draws on the depth structures of each religion. If indeed religions are like languages then we are likely to evolve to have one language with several dialects and one religion using several foundations. This group of people is trying to scope out just what that religious structure might be – a courageous project to be sure.

well-worn path wrestling with old fears, and shattering questions in an attempt to develop a faith beyond a magic God. I'm hoping what I've gleaned might help point the way for others. Here's what you can expect.

Sources for a Conversation

This book is based on a series of sermons I preached at the First Presbyterian Church San Rafael during the season of Lent in 2013. The title of the series was *"Evolution and Christian Faith."*

In the Foreword my friend, Marc Gafni,[11] described a vision for religious dialogue grounded in an Integral World Spirituality framework. It will become clear just what that means as we proceed, but let me say here that Marc's commitment to laying hold of the depth structures that lie at the core of the world's religious traditions is inspiring. It is important to understand that he is not saying that all the world's religions are saying the same thing. To the contrary, it is more that they are all dealing with the same issues but approaching them from different directions. In fact it is the different ways these depth structures are experienced that give each religion its unique and beautiful character. If we can get at the core structures within each of our traditions, see how they unfold, and provide an understanding of our faiths beyond the inevitable modernist deconstruction, we have an opportunity to offer wisdom and insight to one another while remaining faithful to our own tradition. This is what Marc referred to as a "dual-citizenship" model of faith. Marc lives within an Orthodox Jewish tradition. Another friend of ours, Sally Kempton, lives within a Hindu tradition. I am grateful to both; each has offered me deep insight into what it means to be Christian. I hope that I've offered them something in return. Our conversations rather than challenging me to leave my faith, instead deepen my decidedly Christian faith.

---

11. http://www.marcgafni.com

I tell the reader this because the first five chapters of this book are an unfolding of the Unique Self dharma from within a Christian context. The Unique Self teaching, which Dr. Gafni offered in his book, *Your Unique Self: The Radical Path to Personal Enlightenment,* provides a framework for an Integral World Spirituality. I won't be footnoting every instance; that would become tedious. But the reader should know I will be referring to Dr. Gafni's Unique Self teachings throughout the book, particularly in the first section, and in many cases I will be using the language he has developed to describe them. This book owes his extraordinary work a deep debt, for it has inspired me as I've sought to describe a Christian faith beyond a magic God.

I seek to cast a Christian vision for what God is doing in the midst of an evolving creation and what our role in it all might be. In order to cast that vision, I will be interpreting or reinterpreting Christian texts. That has been the way of theological conversation for thousands of years. When I look at the Hebrew and Christian scriptures[12] I see a record of a thousands of years-long conversation about the nature of the Divine and our interaction with the Divine. The Christian scriptures are reinterpreting the Hebrew scriptures from within a different worldview and context. I am profoundly sorry that these two traditions ever split apart and sorrier still for the horrifying treatment Jews have received at the hands of Christians throughout the centuries. I am continuing the long conversation that began in the texts of Torah and continues to this day all over the world.

---

12. I deliberately do not call them the Old and New Testaments since the very name implies that the Christian testament, or covenant, with God supersedes the Hebrew covenant. It implies that Christian faith is more evolved than Hebrew faith. Nonsense. Perhaps that made some little sense from within a traditional mythic point of view, a point of view characterized by exclusive claims on truth, but the time has long since past for us to jettison such arrogant notions.

The Structure of the Book

The first section of the book is effectively a Christian exposition of Unique Self teachings. These teachings are an effort to offer a framework for spiritual transformation that derives from the depths of the worlds' great traditions. I believe they offer one starting point for reconstructing the religious traditions after their inevitable modernist deconstruction. Our culture is in desperate need of such a framework if we are to take the next step in our evolution without completely corrupting our environment and annihilating one another with increasingly clever weapons. To borrow a business term, the Unique Self dharma reduces the cost of discovery for each of the traditions as they evolve beyond a postmodern stage of development. For many years I've been on the hunt for a reconstructed understanding of Christianity that can drive us to become more of who we are created to be. Marc is on to something here.

The second section addresses certain classical, Christian, theological issues, including the nature and authority of Scripture itself, the doctrine of the Trinity, the doctrine of atonement, the nature and efficacy of prayer, and the nature of sin. These topics come up all the time when I find myself in conversation with people wrestling out their faith in a modern world. The second section of the book deals with each of those questions in turn.

The third section of the book is a call to action, a summary call to live a life that reflects the creative love of God. This love is more than just a feeling. It is nothing less than the power driving evolution itself.

Finally for almost fifteen years now my wife has been asking me, "How? How are we supposed to engage in growth and development in the presence of God?" Because she so graciously and persistently raises this question, I contemplate and preach about it more than I otherwise would. She is most certainly my superior on this subject. Therefore I've asked Barbara, a therapist for twenty years, who with her colleague

Claire Molinard has developed a Unique Self Coaching process, to write an Afterword about how we are to live in the joy of God's presence.

I have come to know the love she offers, a love that challenges me over and over, never letting me accept or be satisfied with an imaginary faith, is a love sourced in the power that unfolds creation. It is unfathomable and yet real. Only such a love can address a world in outrageous pain. The reality of that love is what we seek together.

PART I
UNIQUE SELF AS SEEN THROUGH THE CHRISTIAN SCRIPTURES

Each of the world's major religious traditions works to shed light on the nature of "God," and God's interaction with creation. In doing so each creates a context of meaning within which we live our lives. Each one takes a very different approach, defining different issues, answering different questions. The approach each religion takes has significant impact on how its adherents live their lives. But as the world has been made smaller by our ability to communicate, and our capacity to investigate the thought world and rituals that make up virtually every religion in the world, we've been able to discern differences but also coherence among them. The mistake has been to try either to reduce each religion to a kind of "lowest common denominator" in an effort to discover the "truth" at the heart of it all or to claim the exclusive truth of one's own chosen religious path.

There is a third way. Each religious tradition offers deep

and profound insight from within its own context. Even the adherents to each religious tradition haven't plumbed the depths of their own faith; none of us has arrived at a place of perfection. We all long for transformation and change. What I have found is that if we approach each other not only with respect, but with a genuine curiosity and with an open heart, we can be challenged by one another such that our faith is deepened within our own tradition. Talking to a Buddhist who is practiced in her tradition helps me to practice my own decidedly Christian faith more deeply.

In order to have these conversations though, we need some frame of reference that can facilitate this generative conversation. I believe that Dr. Marc Gafni's work on Unique Self provides us with just such a frame of reference. The first part of this book seeks to be in conversation with this frame of reference from within the Christian Scriptures.

So what does Marc mean when he speaks of a Unique Self? At heart, the Unique Self teachings claim that each one of us possesses a unique story of infinite value, each one of us is a gorgeous expression of the love-intelligence of the universe. But that begs the question, "What happens to us?" Why don't we live as though that is true? The answer is that we humans develop a case of mistaken identity. It is part and parcel of the human condition at this point in our evolution. Spiritual masters from across the traditions have been saying this for centuries. We mistakenly conclude that we are separate selves – "skin-encapsulated egos," as Alan Watts called us. We are disconnected or divided from the source of love, the source of creative power that animates creation. Separated from the love intelligence that animates creation we are lost, caught up in our own fear. This is the source of outrageous, mind numbing, horrifying pain in the world—the stuff that explodes our hearts in outrage when we allow ourselves to glimpse it.

This condition of separation is what the world's religious traditions address, each in their own unique way. They use different language and sometimes different approaches, but each moves the faithful to let go of this sense of separation, the separate self, and come to know the One. They encourage us to discover the truth that there is no separation, there is no "other," for we are in fact a True Self and the total number of true selves is one! When we wake up to this reality we are waking up to our being. Eastern religious traditions often refer to this as "enlightenment," Marc calls it "sanity," because if a person does not know who she is, she is insane.

This is wonderful as far as it goes, removing the separation between us and the Divine is surely a necessary first step, but let's take this one step further. If it is true that our being is known in True Self and the total number of true selves is one, if waking up to that is the recovery of sanity, then how come this idea of enlightenment, this denial of the separate self, hasn't caught on in the world? Answer: we have an intuition that there is something very wrong with it. Marc likes to say, "Of course there's something wrong with that, it has taken creation 13.82 billion years to make a Sam, or Zion, or Claire, why on earth would we want to get rid of them and see them absorbed into the One?" It just doesn't feel right. Something is missing.

This is "enlightenment" from the perspective of the Eastern traditions, but Western enlightenment has always come at these issues from a different angle. In the West the "Enlightenment" was all about individual freedom, individual self-actualization. At one level the two seem diametrically opposed, but this does not have to be the case. What happens if we transcend both of these traditions but include each in our understanding of human conscious development? Marc believes it is correct to say there is only one True Self, it is essential for us to realize that we are not separate selves, skin-encapsulated egos. But it is equally true that each one of us has a unique perspective on that one True Self. Each one of us is a unique expression of that One. We are each a Unique Self. Alfred North Whitehead spoke of the "seamless coat of the universe," Marc says, "Yes, the coat of the universe is indeed seamless, but it is not featureless!"

This is tricky business of course. For thousands of years both Eastern and Western mystics have shown us how clever we can be at fooling ourselves into thinking that our separate self is our enlightened self. We would not want to deny that for one moment. It is true that the separate self is relentless in its pursuit to keep hold of our lives and unless we are able to dismantle the separate self we remain cut off from the Source of all that is. But we would also be loath to deny the irreducible beauty and value of each and every Unique Self in creation, each one of us infinitely valuable, a puzzle piece in the vast puzzle of the Universe. No one is extra!

That constitutes a thumbnail sketch of the Unique Self dharma. It is this frame of reference I'll engage throughout the chapters of this book.

Chapter 1

Power to Become Children of God

In the beginning was the Logos and the Logos was oriented towards God. The Logos was God. He was in the beginning oriented towards God. All things came into being through him and without him not one thing came into being. What has come into being with him is life and the life was the light of all people. That light shines in the darkness and the darkness did not overcome it. There was a man who was sent from God. His name was John. He came as a witness to testify to this light so that all might believe that through him. He himself was not the light but he came to testify to the light. The true light which enlightens everyone was coming into the world. He was in the world and the world came into being through him and yet the world did not know him. He came to what was his own and his own people did not receive him. But to all who received him, who trusted in his name, he gave power to become children of God who were born not of blood, or of the will of the flesh, or the will of human beings, but of God. And the Logos became enfleshed and made camp among us and we have seen his glory, the glory as of a parents' only son full of grace and truth. John testified to him and cried out, "This was he of whom I said, he who comes after me ranks ahead of me, because he was before me." From his fullness we have all received grace upon grace. The

> *law indeed was given thorough Moses. Grace and trust came through Jesus the Christ. No one has ever seen God. It is God the only son who is close to the parents' heart, who has made God known.*
>
> John 1:1-8

The prologue to the Gospel according to John is a key text for our culture's understanding of Christianity. It begins, "In the beginning was the Word" or "the Logos." John wants to crack open our imagination, and our hearts, to a most astonishing reality: each of us is a unique expression of the dynamic power that is unfolding creation's evolutionary story towards the good, the true, and the beautiful. To put it another way: you are a unique expression of the love intelligence creating the universe.

Some say the concept of Logos held all the philosophical content of the entire Greek language. For the Greeks, down at the root of reality, was Logos. Logos held the patterns that structured creation. So when John used the word "Logos" to describe Jesus, the Christ, the One who enters into creation to redeem it, he was drawing from a rich philosophical landscape.

But John had more than the structure of creation in mind when he used that word. The Hebrew Scriptures formed and informed John. His prologue reaches back to the creation poem at the beginning of Genesis, the first book of Torah. Torah envisions a dynamic role for the Word of God. *"In the beginning when God created the heavens and the earth, the earth was a formless void and darkness covered the face of the deep while a wind from God swept over the waters. Then God said, 'Let there be light,' and there was light."*[13] God spoke *words* and brought creation into being; God speaks throughout creation's becoming. God's *Word* in the stories

---

13. Genesis 1:1-3.

of the Hebrew scriptures, is dynamic, creative, and powerful, so when John said, "In the beginning was the Word," he was drawing from the heart of the Israelite tradition. He was talking about the Word that brings creation into being.

But John had still more in mind when he chose the word "Logos." His goal wasn't simply to offer us a cognitive grasp of the Christ; he wanted us to know Logos, he wanted us to live into, or up to, our relationship with Logos. And so he consciously set Logos in conversation with the Wisdom tradition of the Hebrew Scriptures. The Wisdom Literature[14] in the Hebrew texts isn't simply a set of disembodied ideas, axioms, or proverbs. No, this is instructions for life derived from the foundational structures of creation, the patterns that connect, and this Wisdom, or in Hebrew, *Hochma*, was personal. Often described as Lady Wisdom, she was understood as alive and relational. Right from the beginning of time she is an interdependent character who stands with God in the midst of the creative process. She is an agent of God's dynamic strength and creative power. When we listen to Hochma speak in the eighth chapter of Proverbs, and then read John's prologue, we hear echoes and resonance between the texts. We see the reflection of *Hochma* in the Logos. *Hochma* speaks:

> *"The Lord created me at the beginning of his work,*
> *the first of his acts of long ago.*
> *Ages ago I was set up,*
> *at the first, before the beginning of the earth.*
> *When there were no depths I was brought forth,*
> *when there were no springs abounding with water.*
> *Before the mountains had been shaped,*
> *before the hills, I was brought forth—* . . ."[15]

For John, this same interdependent character, this agent of God's creative power, is at the most fundamental level what

---
14. The Wisdom Literature of the Bible includes Proverbs, Job, Ecclesiastes, and in the Apocrypha, Sirach and the Wisdom of Solomon.
15. Proverbs 8:22-24.

is real. This *Hochma* is known in the patterns we see running through the creative process itself. John's conviction is that the Logos is by nature oriented towards perfect union with true presence, always moving toward union with what is real.

John's Gospel is written to tell us how this Logos/Hochma interpenetrates creation in a human being, Jesus the Christ. But more important, once we come to understand the creative hope inherent in this story, we are to realize that it is paradigmatic of how Logos interpenetrates each and every one of us! That means this Gospel is about you; this Gospel is about me. It is the story of Logos made incarnate in Jesus, and in you, and in me. That reality impacts every moment of our lives. So we turn our attention to just how this good news is relevant in this outrageously painful world. We see how it addresses the human condition head on.

The human condition leaves a little something to be desired. I mean take the words "I love you," for instance. They're words of intimacy, of closeness and warmth and security. And yet what do we mean when we say them? One would hope we would mean, "I want the very best for you. I'll commit my life to ensuring yours is greater, more beautiful, more inspired." And yet all too often "I love you" means "I'm glad that you are fulfilling my needs right now."

Many years ago my first wife was dying of breast cancer. As we went through a seemingly endless series of crises together we took part in a support group. We learned that during the depths of that relentless disease it is very common for couples to split apart. We called it the "Newt Gingrich Syndrome."[16] Of course each situation is different, but people tend to withdraw from one another during crises like this. It rarely ends in divorce but the withdrawal shows up in other ways. For instance, it was rare to see husbands at the chemo

---

16. Newt Gingrich, we read at the time, left his wife while she was being treated for cancer.

infusion center. Even if, like my wife and I, a couple didn't want the drift apart to happen, you still found it happening.

It happened to us. I'll never forget the day Deb came downstairs and said, "I've found another lump." I knew right then and there that it was only a matter of time, that it was over. My first reaction should have been, "Oh honey, I'm so sorry," and in fact I probably did give her a hug, but my brain wasn't doing that. My brain was thinking: what am I going to do without her income? (She was the major breadwinner.) How am I going to raise these children? And I found that until I could settle my heart down, until I could work out how to take care of my own needs and the needs of our children, it was very difficult for me to open my heart and really focus on taking care of her needs.

I can forgive myself for my response. I did better than many and worse than some others. There's a limit to how much a human being can deal with, how much fear it can cope with. We came closer together later and I certainly cared for her until the end but "I love you?" I'm thinking I fell short. We all do.

That fear we feel, the one that makes us contract, impacts many areas of our lives. This human instinct isn't just about life and death crises. Isn't that what's at the heart of this seemingly endless financial crisis? I don't know a lot about money, but what I do know is that the financial system, the distribution of money, is built on relationships of trust. The green piece of paper I carry around in my wallet has no inherent value. The only value it has is the value you and I agree it has. The more trust vanishes from human society, the more distant we become from one another; the more isolated we feel, the less we trust that relationship. As the relational trust breaks down, our trust in the value of that money breaks down; we become afraid. We seek ways to get more and more money in an effort to fight off the fear – to gain what control we can over our lives. But without the trust, any control we might have is elusive. Fear takes hold and impacts behavior. We try to put our hands on as much as we can get. There is no longer such a thing as "enough." We try to anesthetize ourselves to the loneliness and the fear and so we consume. It is that fear and contraction that drives an unjust, unstable monetary system.

Such fear has far-reaching implications. It's what produces a great deal of the violence in the world. Some time ago I read a study that discovered when a human being is hit, when you're struck, you register the punch as being harder than it actually is. You inflate the power of the punch. When we respond with an "equal hit" it turns out not to be equal at all, for when we return the punch we return it not matching the force of the punch we received, but rather matching our inflated sense of how hard we've been hit. We are wired to escalate the violence! It's a vicious cycle. The first person feels your return punch harder than it actually was and retaliates in kind with an increase in the amount of violence. If it's not checked, the violence spins out of control.

We human beings are neurologically built for violence and cruelty. Throughout history the human imagination has been employed to produce the most horrific cruelty and suffering possible. Philosopher Rene Girard's work shows us that violence is so integral to the human psyche that religion itself had to be invented in order to curb violence whenever people came together in community. It stunning and we've never been able to figure out how to break free of it. It's as though fear has infected us and covered us with a crust of violence so thick we cannot see through it.

Yes, the human condition leaves a little something to be desired. *Worse still . . . we think the situation is static, don't we?* We think that nothing can change it. As my father would say, "It has always been thus." Though most of us don't believe in the concept of original sin, the idea that we are born evil, I think we do tacitly believe in something pretty similar. We assume that the way we are is the way we are. I'm not suggesting that the human condition can be changed with ease, but to believe that we cannot change at all itself perpetuates the human condition.

Harder still is that we seem more comfortable with the idea that the human condition is static than we are with the sometimes painful, yet dynamic reality, that we can change, that change can, and does in fact, occur. It occurs through the process of evolution, through a process that moves from death to new life, from cross to resurrection, if you will. That is how we evolve—from death to new life, from cross to resurrection.

This is the first time I've brought up evolution. People talk about a tension between Christian faith and the concept of an evolving universe. Tension? Not from where I sit. As far as I'm concerned Christian faith and evolution are two sides of the same coin! We'll say more about this later, but cross and resurrection – the central concepts of our faith – describe the process of evolution. They describe God's move from the death of the old into the surprising creation of what's new. Relying on that power we can break out of the static nature of the human condition and move towards a dynamic new reality.

This is what the Gospel of John is saying! The Gospel tells the story of the Logos, the creative drive or power that interpenetrates creation, always growing, always evolving, always moving forever towards the presence of God. That's our hope.

The Logos became flesh and lived among us.[17] It always has become flesh. It always has lived among us. For 13.82 billion years and perhaps longer, the Logos has become flesh because the creative power of God moves into creation in just that way – interpenetrating the creation, unfolding creation from within us.

But let's be clear here: for John the role of Logos is more than acting as an agent of God's creative power. Logos reveals the reality of God's way of being in creation and in so doing our conscious minds are lifted above the self-involved, instinct-driven condition of our lives. John is waking us up to a new reality. The Logos is enfleshed in the Christ but the story is not told so you'll know it happened to Jesus. Rather,

---

17. John 1:14.

it is told to show us the new way, to reveal to us our true nature as what he calls "children of God." For just as Jesus is "Son of God," so we too are "children of God." Again, these are terms that meant something to the author of John, that point to some reality from within his own worldview. We'll have to consider them for a bit to figure out what they might mean from within our own.

For now let's say that it means we are so intimately interpenetrated, so intimately empowered, so reflective of the creative process of God, so expressive of the love intelligence of the universe that we can be called children of God. We can be called children of the One who speaks and creates. We are given power to be creative agents or creative expressions of the love that is driving evolution forward.

Consider that at this point in our development human beings understand the evolutionary process that drives creation forward. That means we are self-conscious of our own evolution. The universe has created a mind, the universe has created eyes, the universe has created a heart to know and to feel and to understand itself. We are part of it. Logos, which interpenetrates the whole of reality, is now not so much acting upon us as it is being expressed through us. Did you hear that? *Logos is not so much acting upon us now as it is being expressed through us. This is what it means to be children of God.* Creation is not static. We are evolving, becoming more perfect expressions of the love of God.

John is telling us that this is who we are. We are children of God. The story of the gospel, though, the story of our lives interpenetrated by Logos, is our becoming, our living into this reality.

Throughout John's Gospel the Logos is expressed in Jesus as a paradigm of how Logos is expressed in each human being. Jesus is showing us *the way*. We are called to express this creative power just as Jesus did. *"Very truly, I tell you, the one who believes in me will also do the works that I do and, in fact, will do greater works than these, because I am going to the Father,"* (John 14:12). We are partners in this new and dynamic life. It requires that we live into that life. We do that by following what John calls "the way."

Fourteen times in John's Gospel he refers to "the way," the earliest name for Jesus' followers. Before they were called Christians, they were called people of "the way." This "way," is a spiritual journey. Jesus is our guide. The first step along "the way" is union with the source of all that is, with being itself. This can seem foreign at first, difficult to grasp, especially in a western culture that thinks of "enlightenment" in terms of the individual. But stay with me, please, just until I suggest there is something more to "the way" than reaching a moment of mystical union, because we'll find that "the way" will then take a surprising turn.

But let's look first at this union with Logos. Throughout John's Gospel Jesus makes the mystical declaration, "I AM." He is reaching back to the origins of his own tradition, because his understanding of "I AM-ness" was born in Torah, in the heart of the teaching we have received and continue to receive from the Jews.

"I AM." The biblical text says it over and over again. From the burning bush in Exodus to the sayings of Jesus, it points toward what is real: we are One. This is a Oneness that knows no "other" to be complete. This is the True Self. "I AM," Jesus said, and since the relationship Jesus has with God is paradigmatic of the relationship we are called to have, this is the first step along our "way." But what might this Oneness, this True Self mean? It sounds more like the mystical experiences people report as they remove themselves from the real world and sit on the proverbial mountain top, and there is certainly something of the truth in that, but there is more to it.

Dr. King once reflected on the "argument" God had with

Moses at the burning bush. [18]He drew a contrast between God, the I AM, and, (though he didn't use this vocabulary), each of our separate selves. Each separate self can claim, "I am," but following that statement we have to add a qualifier. We can say, "I am," but we have to add, "because my parents met so many years ago, got married and started a family." But God is different. "God, the power that holds the universe in the palm of his hand, is the only being that can say, "I AM," and put a period there . . . "[19] This is the nature of Oneness: I AM with no qualifier.

As separate selves describing the truth of who we are, we can say, "I am," but inevitably we have to add, "because I had this experience, or that lover, or made that awful mistake. I am because I live with this shame buried so deep I can't even see it, or this set of talents that earn me praise, or this set of wounds. But Jesus does not leave us alone in our separate self. As Jesus directs us along "the way" he calls us to let go of those qualifiers and say with him, "I AM."

We need not be identified or attached to our shame, or our wounds. Even our gifts aren't ours to brag about; they are gifts. When we are able to do this, when we drop the qualifiers holding us back and taking us down, we reach the Oneness Jesus calls for; we come to the realization of True Self. As the attachments are broken, even attachments to our talents, we discover that we are free, free from our separate, false self, free from this qualified view of who we are. Instead we find ourselves united, embraced, living as the One True Self.

Just as Jesus is the I AM, so too are we. Each of us can say, "I am so clearly loved by God that all of what has qualified me falls away. What's left is "I AM;" True Self. Each one of us can say "I AM," and put a period at the end of the sentence. The question is, why would we want to?!

As my friend Marc likes to say, "It took 13.82 billion

---

18. Exodus 3
19. Dr. Martin Luther King. Jr., *A Knock at Midnight*, edited by Clayborne Carson and Peter Holloran (New York, New York, Warner Books, 1998), 135

years for the universe to form you and now you're supposed to give it up and be absorbed into the One True Self? There's something wrong with that picture," which is why the next step along "the way" knocks me out. For this Oneness, this One True Self, this pinnacle of Eastern enlightenment is limited.

Do you ever wonder why enlightenment hasn't really caught on here in the west? It hasn't captured our culture's imagination and that's because "enlightenment" in the West typically refers instead to the ultimate realization of the individual rather than to our ultimate interconnectedness. But John is pointing the way towards synthesizing these two visions of enlightenment. It is true he proclaims that in order to live and to love, in order to create and to thrive, we must let the false self, the false sense of separation fall away. Only then can we arrive at the union Jesus describes, and be completely sourced by the power of creation.

This is the extraordinary good news of John's Gospel. We are not living in a static condition. We are not living separate from the power of love that animates the universe. No, we are One and so we are sourced, empowered, inspired, even obligated to live out the life of Logos in our own unique way. That is our destiny; that is our purpose. We are not static false selves destined to remain the same— dismal, broken, forever and ever, amen. No, we are destined to become unique creatures who reflect the reality of God's love in a new life. That is what the Gospel of John is pointing to with its stories and images and symbols.

You are called to be a Unique Self, to become a unique expression of the love of God. Follow the way and you are given power to become Children of God. If we let this way form us, we begin to break free of the selfish finitude that keeps us from loving one another. Justice begins to flourish as we live a life that trusts in the presence of this abundant creative power. A life entrusted to Logos can break the cycle of violence; it is an answer to a world in outrageous pain.

An evolutionary Christianity is realistic about the enormity of that task, but hopeful too, for it recognizes the power of creation unfolding within us, driving that transformative change. For the creative power of love does not so much act upon us as it is expressed through us.

We live in a dynamic world and you and I have the capacity to make it more whole, more beautiful, closer to the presence of God because the Logos of God expresses God's love and power through us. That is the good news and it demands our response.

Chapter 2

We Are in This Together

During those days, (that is to say those days when Jesus was wandering through the countryside, healing people and teaching), *during those days he went out to the mountain to pray and he spent the night in prayer oriented towards God. When the day came he called his disciples and chose twelve of them whom he named apostles,* (that is people who are sent). *Simon whom he named Peter, and his brother Andrew, and James and John and Phillip and Bartholomew and Matthew and Thomas and James the son of Alphaeus and Simon who was called the Zealot and Judas son of James and Judas Iscariot who became a traitor.*

Luke 6:12-16

I feel pretty fortunate to live in Marin County. It's rare indeed that I meet somebody who lives here who is just oh so sorry that they live here and wishes they could move somewhere else—you know, back to Iowa maybe? I just don't meet people who long to leave this place. It's gorgeous. The weather's great, the economy is reasonably solid, there's a lot of opportunity here. In fact one of the opportunities we have, one that I have taken up in the last year, is to attend the Marin Speaker's Series.

I recently heard Zanny Minton-Beddoes, the economics editor for the *Economist* magazine, speak about the global financial picture. Specifically, she'd been talking about what's happening in China. Right now they have five young people for every one adult, but twenty years from now it's going to be different. They are going to have two young people for every one older adult. We can only imagine what that will do to an economy, to lose that many jobs.

She talked about the mobility gap between rich and poor as well. If you are rich, then your children are almost certain to remain wealthy, and if you are poor your children are almost certain to remain poor. The American Dream is bankrupt. She pointed to a cause for that: the way our schools are funded. They are funded by property taxes, so it figures that locations with high property values will have plenty of money for education. Places where that's not the case? Well, they're out of luck. In the last thirty years the gap between the test scores of rich kids and poor kids has increased by forty percent.

So Zanny was talking about these unstable, unjust conditions all over the world from Europe and Asia, to South America, and on and on. Then the question came. "We are living in Marin County where unemployment is low, housing prices are strong; we live in the bubble you talked about. Why shouldn't we just enjoy it and not worry about the other people in the world?"

Really? There it was, the worst of Marin County stereotypes on display for everyone to see.

Our speaker stumbled for the first time in her entire talk. Then she regrouped, and spoke of how we are all interconnected; she offered that as a reason to care. The reason? Enlightened self-interest. The fact that the Chinese economy may get into serious trouble over the next three decades is a serious problem not just for them, but for us in the U.S. as well because it's the Chinese economy that puts the floor underneath the bond market, Ms. Minton-Beddoes explained. If that floor isn't there, then economies all over the world collapse.

She pointed to the facts in this country; we have the same problem as China. There are not enough young people to take care of, or pay for, all the retirees coming through the pipeline. There's not enough money for social security or health care. In circumstances like that we can't just waste young people, leaving some uneducated and others well off. We've got to educate everyone if we're going to make things happen. So she talked about our interconnectedness as a reason to care for others.

If she had known more about Marin, she could have brought it even a bit closer to home. You know that SMART train that has taken so long to approve? The single biggest reason for building it is to provide transportation for immigrants to work here in Marin and care for this aging population, when they can't afford to live here. Unpleasant though it may be, so the reasoning goes, it is better for Marin residents than not having the train. Interconnected, that was her reason to care for others – enlightened self-interest.

But I looked around the audience, (and she made a comment about this too), and saw that a lot of the audience were of retirement age. I was one of the youngest people in the room and I'm 58. If that horrifying question came from one of the older people in the room, then enlightened self-interest, understanding that we're all interconnected, won't be an adequate answer at all. It will take twenty years for some of these economic disasters to unfold. What difference would it make for someone older? Enlightened self-interest won't work as a motivator. So what do we say? How do we answer the question? My answer comes from an understanding of the evolutionary nature of creation.

I'm exploring the claim that the cross and the resurrection beautifully describe the evolutionary process, that is, the way evolution operates,. Evolutionary meta-theorists and the Scriptures within which the Christian conversation about God takes place, both come up with very similar answers to the question, "Why should we care for others?" It will take us a little while to get there, but the answer to that question has to do with the direction in which creation is moving. Creation is moving towards unity, not uniformity you understand, but unity. It's in the nature of things.

The small but I think representative piece of Luke's Gospel I put at the beginning of this chapter, like the Gospel as a whole, is about driving towards unity. The text I chose, the moment Jesus selected twelve apostles, is a key moment in the story of Jesus seeking to expand his reach and join others into a new community, a new vision of humanity. The antagonists in Luke's story are the Pharisees along with the religious hierarchy. As characters in Luke's story they exemplify what I'd call an ethnocentric worldview.

Carol Gilligan of Harvard University has done significant work in mapping the moral development of human beings. We move from being egocentric where the circle of people we care about amounts to our self and maybe those who are taking care of us. At some point we grow up, we evolve, and our circles of care expand to include the community of which we're a part. That can include everything from our high school and the San Francisco Giants to our ethnic group or our entire nation. These are the people with whom we can make common cause. There are those on the inside and those on the outside.

The Pharisees in Luke's story are operating at an ethnocentric level of development. They don't much care about the broader community of nations. (Sounds a lot like Zanny Minton-Beddoes' questioner, does it not? That person's circle of care did not seem to extend beyond his or her own community—-lovely, wealthy, Marin County.)

Because the Pharisees and religious hierarchy were taking this ethnocentric worldview, because their circle of care did not extend beyond their own people, Luke's Jesus is very concerned that the nation of Israel is not living into its promise; they are not living into their covenant, into their purpose to become "*a blessing to all the families of the earth*" (Genesis 12:1-3). [Emphasis mine.] Jesus understands it this way and he's deeply concerned that the existing political hierarchy of Israel has turned away from that call. He is so concerned in fact that in the story Luke tells he's looking to reconstitute the people of God. That is why he chose twelve apostles; twelve apostles corresponding to the twelve tribes of Israel.

In the story, Jesus chooses twelve because he has every intention of starting a new reign, a new kingdom—of God. This reign that comes from God is moving towards greater unity, greater inclusion. Jesus envisions a new Israel whose circle of care expands to take in all families or nations of the earth. He is looking to develop what Carol Gilligan called a world-centric worldview.

That theme is thoroughgoing in Luke's Gospel. It shows up in the first sermon Jesus preached. In chapter four Jesus goes into the synagogue at Nazareth and reads some of the most hopeful portions of the prophet Isaiah. "The Spirit of the Lord is upon me, because he's anointed me to bring good news to the poor. He has sent me to proclaim release to the captives and recovery of sight to the blind, to let the oppressed go free," and then concludes his reading by saying that he's been sent "to proclaim the year of the Lord's favor" (Luke 4:19). These are longed for words of hope for a people living under the thumb of Roman occupation. Jesus applies them to his own ministry. The people were a bit suspicious, though. First of all that's quite a claim, especially from a hometown boy. But there was something else that made them very suspicious. He didn't finish Isaiah's sentence! Jesus ended with, "to proclaim the year of the Lord's favor;" but the passage goes on to say, "and the day of vengeance of our God" (Isaiah 61:2). They were waiting to hear about how God would bring the hammer down on their enemies, the Romans, but Jesus didn't give them that.

Then, after getting some resistance from this home-town crowd, Jesus explains himself by retelling the Bible stories about Zarephath, the widow Elijah helped, and Naaman, the Syrian general that Elisha cured of leprosy. When Jesus did this he was deliberately referring to two Gentiles. In fact he was referring to the only Gentiles who are depicted as receiving God's healing power, in the entire Hebrew Bible. Very early in Luke's story Jesus was showing the people that God's plan and purpose includes all peoples. Jesus is calling his people to expand their circle of care, to live out their call of blessing to all the families of the earth. He pointedly reveals the care God has for all people, not just them. He's pointing towards unity. He's *world*-centric if you will, not *ethno*-centric.

There are other ways in which the Jesus of Luke moves in the direction of unity. He seems to have a particular concern or sensitivity for the feminine. That doesn't mean that the author of Luke was a feminist or that he was not enmeshed in a patriarchal culture. He was, and feminist Bible scholars have appropriately pointed that out. Nevertheless, when compared to the other gospels, the concerns of women are raised again and again in Luke's story, always with an eye towards unity.

There is further evidence of Luke's interest in unity. For it's in this gospel that the story of the Good Samaritan is told. The Good Samaritan is called "good" because when a victim of robbery was left for dead at the side of the road, it was he, a foreigner, a Samaritan, and not the Priest or the Levite, who cared for the victim. The Samaritan understood what it meant to be a neighbor, to bring unity to the world.

Luke more than the other gospel writers carries a deep concern for the poor. That concern first manifests itself in the Magnificat, that wonderful song Mary sang as she imagined what a wonder it was to carry the Messiah in her womb. She sang knowing this child would bring hope to the poor, would reverse the power structure so that the poor might be lifted up—so that the mobility gap might be narrowed, so to speak.

Finally, it is Luke who cares about anyone or anything that is lost. In the fifteenth chapter of his gospel he tells the stories of the lost son (the "prodigal son" we sometimes call him), the lost sheep, and the lost coin. Each of these stories drives home the point: no one is left behind.

That's always the way it is in the Gospel of Luke. Jesus is working to create the reign of God, a new nation, a new land of promise, by bringing unity to the world, by drawing people together instead of splitting people apart. As he marched steadily towards Jerusalem, as though fate itself had determined his destiny, he gathered more and more people into the project that unites, and the Spirit of God continued to drive it forward.

Throughout Luke, each time Jesus prayed, some new move would carry this good news forward, the new nation would grow, the promise and the hope of freedom would grow. It moved from Nazareth to Jerusalem as the Gospel of Luke unfolds. Then, right when you think something like the cross, the crucifixion of the new nation's founder, might stop it in its tracks, a new life emerges from the grave. This is an essential characteristic, the central characteristic of the gospel and it is equally characteristic of evolution's meandering movement through history. New life emerges from death.

Three things or movements characterize any evolutionary step forward: novelty, transcendence and inclusion, and increasingly complex self-organization. These moves apply to the resurrection of Jesus in Luke's story. When he rose from the dead, he did not rise to the same kind of life he had lived. What emerged was surprising, novel. Second, his new life transcended the life he had lived with his disciples, but was also included in the new emergent life. Disciples recognized their risen Lord. Finally, it was a life of increasing complexity. The new life that emerged from the grave was God's next move forward. Crucifixion ultimately could not stop the movement towards unity, towards shalom.

Each time an obstacle stood in the way of the new nation's growth, it was removed. The project continued to move forward in the sequel to Luke, the Acts of the Apostles. In that work, the new nation, a nation seeking the unity and the blessing of all people, traveled from Jerusalem to the capital of the known world, Rome.

Just as in Luke, when something blocked the progress of unity in Acts, the Spirit of God, that which drives evolution forward, moved through the obstacle and the new community continued on. In Acts you may remember that the issue that threatened to divide this nascent community was an argument about whether one needed to become a Jew first in order to be included in the new promise of God's reign. This was a hugely divisive issue in the early church. The Apostle Peter faced the issue in a dream. The Holy Spirit used the dream to send Peter to baptize the Roman centurion, Cornelius. Peter was so clear that this was the will of the Spirit that when a leadership council of this new Jewish sect was called to settle the issue, Peter's voice carried the day. It was decided that Jews and Gentiles would live side by side in this new reign of God. Unity is the promise of the future in Luke and Acts.

The history of this issue in the early church is complex. I have described what happened from the perspective of Luke's Gospel. What actually happened was far more complex. But the point stands: Luke's Gospel recognizes that the direction of God's creation is towards unity!

So, what might the text offer as at least the beginnings of an answer to our question, "Why should we care for others?" In part because the direction of evolution, reflective of the purpose of creation, is towards unity. Luke looks at the character of Jesus' ministry and opens our eyes to the work of a God who, as the author of Colossians put it, "binds everything together in perfect harmony" (Colossians 3:14). We see the direction of creation towards unity in Luke, but we see it in the work of evolutionary theorists as well.

Ever since Lynn Margulis' landmark 1967 paper, *On the Origin of Mitosing [Eukaryotic] Cells*, evolutionary biologists have moved away from a model of evolution that sees only the dynamics of competition. Her work saw something remarkable in the transformation of bacterium into the first nucleated cells, the origin of animal life. As ancient bacterium were under ecological stress having polluted their environment, instead of competing for the resources needed to maintain the species such that the strongest would survive, instead she found that "the nucleated cell—an entirely new life form about a thousand times larger than an individual bacterium—formed, as the bacteria took on divisions of labor and donated part of their unique genomes to the new cell's nucleus."[20] In short, it was cooperation and unity within the diversity of the bacterium that drove this dramatic moment in evolution forward.

"This process," she went on to say, "whereby tension and hostilities between individuals lead to negotiation and then ultimately to cooperation as a greater unity—is the basic evolutionary process of all life forms on our planet, as I see it."[21]

That's incredible. We live in a world where, as Carter Phipps puts it, "the spoils of evolution go not to the fastest or the smartest but to those who can find the best relationship between creative individuality and cooperative sociality."[22] That is the direction of creation. It is the movement of Spirit. Evolutionary biologists say so. Jesus in Luke's Gospel says so.

The pattern emerges over and over again in the history of evolution. As creation takes each step forward on its evolutionary path, it moves from unity to individuation. Individuation leads to tension or conflict, which, through the process of negotiation and resolution, moves to unity. It's the way things are in an evolutionary world; it's the way things are for bacteria, ants, and for mammals; that includes us.

We see this process of tension between the individual and the cooperative elements bringing us towards unity across the spectrum of human development. Consider our spiritual development. Those who engage in the practice of meditation have long seen the movement back and forth between a sense of our own self-development in relation to God and the apprehension that we live united in God. There is no "other." Paul calls it "union with Christ" (I Corinthians 6:17), for John it is "the way" to unity with the Father, (John 14), and for Solomon it's the call to a relationship so intimate that an

---

20. As quoted in Carter Phipps, *Evolutionaries: Unlocking the Spiritual and Cultural Potential of Science's Greatest Idea*, (San Francisco: HarperCollins, 2012) p. 52.
21. Phipps, Evolutionaries, 53
22. Ibid., 54

intimate sexual relationship best describes it (Song of Songs).

Consider how our bodies work. When we work on our bodies, we recognize they must be healthy for our minds to work at their best. That's because of the unity among the individual cells of our bodies. The health of each cell has an impact on the whole. The split between mind and body is artificial. Consider our economy. We seek a balance between the individual striving of creative souls and the unity that must evolve for any economic system to survive. It's the nature of things.

As we evolve our view of the world, we find the circle that defines who we care about expands. It expands from being egocentric to ethno-centric to world-centric and to kosmo-centric. Once upon a time it was just you and your family to care about, then the tribe, then the nation, and now increasingly we see a worldview emerge that cares for the whole world as a unified system. It is how creation works.

We're still young as a species, so we don't yet have this unity and cooperation thing figured out as well as the ants, for instance, but we are moving in that direction. We're just coming to a place where we are aware of our own evolution, where we are aware of the direction that creation is moving, a direction intuited by the ancients and experimentally observed by the modernists. And so it is that the Gospel of Luke and evolutionary meta-theorists point in the same direction. They suggest that we serve creation's direction and purpose by the care we show for one another. But is this enough? Is this enough of an answer to the person who wanted to know why we should care about people living outside the Marin bubble? I'm going to guess not, for we who are comfortable have little motivation to explore the territory beyond ourselves unless someone or something happens to wake us up.

I wrote earlier that each one of us is a unique expression of the love of God, the creative power of Logos herself. But there is more to it than that – much more. We reflected on that when we talked about the I AM-ness of the Logos in the previous chapter. Your life, your creative juice, is sourced in the Logos and that Logos, is a) the creative power that animates all of creation, and b) what unites us and makes us whole. You are not a separate entity, a skin-encapsulated ego. You are a unique expression of the Logos, of the creative unfolding of all that is. You are an integrated, unique, and essential expression of the One that is moving all things together in perfect harmony. Without you we are not complete; there is no Shalom. We're right at the heart of the answer to our question here.

If a girl sold into sexual slavery in Thailand cannot express the creative power of God as she was made to do, then we are not complete—YOU are not complete. When millions of people lose their jobs or are forced to relocate because sea levels are rising, then each of their essential, integrated, unique expressions of God's creative intention will be distorted. As a result YOUR life will be incomplete. That's just reality; it's in the nature of the way things actually are. Which brings us back to the question of why we should care for others when we are enjoying life just fine without considering their plight.

If we are living life as though we are disconnected, we are living in a dead space; we are living a lie. But perhaps I have still failed to convince? *Let me put it another way.* "Why shouldn't we just enjoy it and not worry about the other people in the world?" Honestly, it's because we can't; we just can't. My claim is this: it is impossible for you to enjoy the comfort, the security, the weather, of Marin or any other beautiful place you're lucky enough to live in, without caring for the rest of the world. You may say you're enjoying life, you can suggest that things are going well for you here in Marin, you may even have convinced yourself that such is the case, but I don't believe it, and honest to God, if you spend any time with it I think you'll know you don't believe it either. You'll know that when you are trying to live that life, deep down, you feel empty, miserable, or worse, you may think I have no idea what I'm talking about. I'm not trying to beat up on you here; I'm trying to awaken you to the incredible joy that comes when you open your heart to the world and start to love.

If you try to live without care for others, if you disconnect yourself from the source of what connects us one to another and gives us life, you will be living a life so empty that it can hardly be called a life at all. When you find yourself alone, in those moments of silence you'll hear the emptiness screaming back at you. We are alive to play our unique part, to offer our unique voice so that we all might be joined together in perfect harmony. Try to avoid that and any spark that lives within you will scream back saying, "I want to live."

Why do you think our lives have become a constant stream of noise, distractions, entertainments, and addictive pleasures? I can't even fill up my gas tank without a television set at the pump telling me that this or that celebrity checked into rehab and is so very sorry to have disappointed all his fans. It's what we have to do to anesthetize the pain. It's like a gag we put on ourselves to silence the screams. Can you live that way? Well sure, you can pretend to, but no, not really. It's miserable. The answer to why we should care about the other is that we cannot actually live life any other way. Waking up to that reality is the first step towards genuine living, the kind of living to which Jesus called his disciples all those years ago.

So how will we respond? Shall we drown out the silence? Or shall we live? That is the question. It may be the question that is staring you down. Will you continue to drown out the painful cries of the other or will you live?

Here's where the culture that has rejected church starts to roll its collective eyes at me. How shall we live a life of purpose? They're suspicious of the church when the question comes up, because the church's answer for way too long has been, "Go to church, listen to preachers tell us we're sinners, then beg forgiveness of a loving God. And rest easy in the knowledge that you'll walk those gold-paved streets one day." Oh my God! I keep wondering how we've gotten our own message so wrong for so long.

But if going to church and begging forgiveness isn't the

answer, then what is? What are we to do? Shall we find a comfortable mountain top and sit for a decade or two until we find enlightenment? No, there's too much at stake for such withdrawal. The reality is that Spirit is on the move; right now, the Spirit is on the move. What's next is emerging. Jesus' call to his disciples is as valid today as it was the moment he called them forth and asked them to live!

You are the unique face of what is true, of that which is whole, of what the Jewish people from whom we come call Shalom. That is who we are in our essence. The good news of the gospel is this: at the level of essence, we are not distorted, hopeless sinners, for God said, "Behold it is very good." No, we are a gorgeous reflection of what is true. Thirteen point eight two billion years from the Big Bang to Shakespeare. We are an integral part of that creative project. The purpose of creation, our purpose, is to become who we really are, to become that which is gorgeous, united, beautiful, and whole.

Most of us reading this are quite fortunate, I presume; the universe has unfolded in a way that places us where it does, with at least enough affluence to provide a computer, the leisure time and the education to read. Enjoying it is part of the deal, but integral to enjoying it is recognizing that we have something to offer the world, a unique offering that only we can give. Integral to enjoying life is taking up the call and responsibility inherent in the beauty we enjoy every day.

My wife and I had several of our son's high school friends over for dinner a few weeks ago. They're all in college now. We asked them what had changed for them since they left home, what they had seen that they didn't see when they were growing up here in Marin. Each one of those young men in his own way said he now knows he comes from privilege, but each also said he knows that with that privilege comes responsibility. Each of them expressed his intention to use his vocation to meet that responsibility. Each one of them was listening to his unique voice, his unique self. *That* was the best of Marin on display.

There is, as my friend Marc Gafni always begins, outrageous pain in the world and the only response to outrageous pain is outrageous love. When we open our hearts, when we recognize that we are not alone but are an essential face of the unity of creation, then we know what life is, then we can live from our connection one to another sourced by the presence of God.

That's why we care for other people. Nothing is complete without you, or them. Spirit can't get the job done without you or them. That's been the message all the way through. That's the message of unity. Unity requires individuals that enjoy the life they have, and enjoyment means applying all of who we are to the creative movement of God's creation.

It can't be done without you. We are in this together.

CHAPTER 3

Ethical Imperative

We find ourselves ethically destitute just when, for the first time, we are faced with ultimacy, the irreversible closing down of the Earth's functioning in its major life systems. Our ethical traditions know how to deal with suicide, homicide, and even genocide; but these traditions collapse entirely when confronted with biocide, the extinction of the vulnerable life systems of the Earth, geoside, the devastation of the earth itself. . . . The human is at a cultural impasse. . . . Radical new cultural forms are needed.[23]

15:29 After Jesus had left that place, [that place being the encounter with the Canaanite woman where he offered blessing and healing to her outside the place of Israel]. After he left that place, Jesus passed along the Sea of Galilee and he went onto a mountain where he sat down. Great crowds came to him and they brought they lame, maimed, lined, mute, many others. They put them at Jesus' feet and he cured them so that they crowds were amazed when they saw the mute speaking and the maimed whole and the lame walking, the blind seeing and they praised the God of Israel.

---

23. Thomas Berry in Carter Phipps, "Evolutionaries," 308.

> *5:1 When Jesus saw the crowds, he went up upon the mountain and after he sat down, his disciples came to him. Then he began to speak and he taught them, saying blessed are the poor in spirit, for theirs is the kingdom of heaven, blessed are those who mourn for they will be comforted, blessed are the meek for they will inherit the earth, blessed are those who hunger and thirst for righteousness for they will be filled. Blessed are the merciful for they will receive mercy, blessed are the pure in heart for they will see God, blessed are the peacemakers for they will be called children of God, blessed are those who are persecuted for righteousness sake, for theirs is the kingdom of heaven, blessed are you when people revile you and persecute you and utter all kinds of evil against you falsely on my account. Rejoice, be glad, for your reward is great in the heavens for in the same way they persecuted the prophets who went before you.*
>
> Matthew 15:29-31, 5:1-12

We have been talking about evolutionary theory and its interface with Christian faith. When you hear the word "evolution," I suspect most people in our culture think, "Yeah I know what that means: that we're descended from apes." If they're slightly more educated, maybe what they think is that we have a common ancestor with the apes, and maybe some people, especially if they're well traveled, know something about the birds and turtles on the Galapagos Islands and evolution. Others who study evolution recognize that the theory is about the evolution of all life. It's just how it works.

You see, evolution moves in steps. Life grows and develops in steps. It responds to stress and it responds to pain. The response transcends the current system. "Lower" or "less-evolved" forms of life are transcended, become more complex.

The complexity is surprising and can't really be predicted – like the property of flow that came from the union of two hydrogen and one oxygen atom. So, single-celled organisms left to their own devices don't survive as well as a group of single-cells in cooperatives. Slime mold is an example of how a single-celled organism has transcended itself by entering into a cooperative arrangement, by including each of the individual organisms that make up the larger whole.[24] It's similar to a book that's made of paragraphs, which are made of words, which are made of letters.

And as that cooperation continues, as evolution proceeds, what we find is that some of those single cells (or at least their progeny) take on a specialized role. Maybe they even get together in groups and perform specialized functions, like eyes for eyesight. It's really quite remarkable. The movement from old to new, from death to new life, is the very same thing as the movement from cross to resurrection. When Jesus rose, it was not as the same old human being, but as a new humanity, one that was more evolved. Like Jesus, we too continue to evolve, internally, culturally, economically, and physically, and Jesus was a part of that process.

So, why does any of this matter? It matters because the world is in outrageous pain and longs for creation's evolutionary response. Spirit is calling to us to be part of that response. That's what Jesus was about. Jesus sought to heal the pain in our first passage in Matthew as he healed the lame, maimed, blind, and the mute. But Jesus was interested in more than healing the body because evolution, the way in which the cosmos is created, concerns itself with more than growth in the body; it is creating all of life. Everything is evolving.

Consider where homo sapiens came from. The species from which we evolved had only a reptilian brain, the brain that responds to fear, that raw sense of protecting life and

---

24. Much of the imagery from this chapter is drawn from the work of Carter Phipps in his excellent work *Evolutionaries: Unlocking the Spiritual and Cultural Potential of the Science's Greatest Idea*, (San Francisco: HarperCollins, 2012), 49 ff.

grabbing hold of what will sustain life. But we are also ancestors of creatures that developed a mammalian brain, able to process emotion. But we developed further. We eventually developed the neo-cortex, that frontal lobe that makes us able to have a sense of self-consciousness.

So, physical evolutions, yes, but it's more than the physical brain that is evolving. It's also our consciousness. Jean Gebser, a German researcher, mapped how cultural consciousness evolved from archaic to magic, to mythic, to mental, and into an integral frame. James Fowler, a researcher at Emory, looked at the way our faiths, our beliefs, evolved from magic into mythic, into a mental state, and from there into a more coherent integral state. Researchers are mapping the evolution of our collective values. Clare Graves, Don Beck and Christopher Cowan have plotted the way our values have evolved. They've mapped how tribal consciousness and values evolved into a mythical consciousness that supports nations, and how that evolved into modern values that provided the engine for industrial growth. We are able to recognize that human beings evolve. Our culture evolves, our internal lives evolve, our brains have evolved, even the structures that hold us together evolve. Once upon a time all we did was go out, hunt and gather, poke around, until finally we figured out that if we plowed and stayed put we would be able to feed ourselves more reliably. That set the stage for invention through which industries came and next the information age.

Human beings evolve internally and externally, as individuals and as a group, and each of these four areas of development affects the others. They evolve together. In fact we get in trouble when evolution gets out of balance – consider a tribal warrior with modern weapons.

What we know is that Spirit drives us forward. Christians describe that work of Spirit as we look through the lens of the Christ. Other religions have other ways, and in fact that's what makes inter-religious dialogue interesting. Challenged by other perspectives, it helps each of us deepen in our own tradition. But for Christians, the Christ nudges us forward towards that moment of complexity, of unity, of shalom. Christ inspires us to become whole, step by step, each step responding to the pain and the dysfunction of the level of development that preceded it.

The world is in outrageous pain. What shall be our response? If the Spirit of God whom we come to know in Scripture is indeed unfolding within us, what shall be our response to this outrageous pain in others? It must be outrageous love. Not a "wrap it up and hold it close" kind of love, but a productive, creative kind of love that seeks to put value into the creation. The creative Spirit and love of God is unfolding within us right now. The world is in outrageous pain and needs our response of love to evolve.

A new step is right on the horizon. At this critical moment in development, consider what's happened to our understanding of the presence of Spirit. Modernism has taken its toll and offered its value. Modernism has done a good job at developing technologies that allow us to become more and more productive, but it has deconstructed any notion about an active presence of God in our lives. Our spiritual development has atrophied. That is a problem because it is the spiritual and religious line of development that gives life its purpose. Without the active presence of God in our lives, without a sense of purpose, we've placed our technological inventiveness at the service of our lusts and desires. In so doing we have brought the world to the brink of ecological destruction.

Even more worrisome is the postmodern deconstruction of truth. "All truth is perspectival," the postmodernist sentiment says. And with that statement we have lost the ability to hold anyone accountable for his behavior. Of course those in power can hold others accountable, but the truly disturbing thing is this: if there is no truth, if there are only competing perspectives about what is true, then whose "perspective on truth" wins? Answer: The one with the biggest gun. That is a recipe for disaster. It creates outrageous pain, pain that demands an immediate response of outrageous love.

Jesus called his disciples to respond to the outrageous

pain of his time. He didn't know the mechanism of evolution, but he understood how to participate in Spirit's creative activity. From the moment the Spirit descended upon him at his baptism, the Spirit was moving his future forward. From the time Spirit drove him into the wilderness to be tested and formed to the moment he gave his life to establish shalom, Spirit was unfolding in his life. Yes, he healed people on the mountainside that day, but he went further and imagined what an evolved world would look like. He could see a human community unified in the presence of God.

Scholars argue about whether or not the beatitudes are intended to set forth a realistic vision of human community. Was Jesus just pointing the way, or was he idealistic enough to expect that community to exist? He meant it to exist. Blessed are those who mourn, blessed are the meek, blessed are the merciful, blessed are the pure in heart, blessed are the peacemakers: with these words Jesus was imagining a world unified in the presence of God, a world that is loved, a world driven by the power of the Spirit of God, a world unfolding within us. Such words call us to live and to love one step larger than we live right now.

So imagine living in that world, in a world where you attend to your own life, to the evolution of your own Spirit, and where you attend to the evolution of the culture around you. Can we finally engage in the marketplace of ideas as though it matters what we think, it matters what is true and what is false? Can we take care of our bodies in a way that makes us more effective? Can we go to work on the structures of this world such that they support unity?

Spirit is calling. We don't know what the next era of the world will be like but it is clear that what emerges will be because the love of God is on the move. And the winds of Spirit are blowing. The days of a deconstructed faith are done. It's time for you and for me to reconstruct our faith because it matters. People are waiting.

CHAPTER 4

Stress Drives Evolution

After he had said this, [Jesus] went on ahead, going up to Jerusalem. When he had come near Bethpage and Bethany, at the place called the Mount of Olives, he sent two of the disciples, saying, Go into the village ahead of you, and as you enter it you will find tied there a colt that has never been ridden. Untie it and bring it here. If anyone asks you, Why are you untying it? just say this, The Lord needs it. So those who were sent departed and found it as he had told them. As they were untying the colt, its owners asked them, Why are you untying the colt? They said, The Lord needs it. Then they brought it to Jesus; and after throwing their cloaks on the colt, they set Jesus on it. As he rode along, people kept spreading their cloaks on the road. As he was now approaching the path down from the Mount of Olives, the whole multitude of the disciples began to praise God joyfully with a loud voice for all the deeds of power that they had seen, saying, Blessed is the king who comes in the name of the Lord! Peace in heaven, and glory in the highest heaven! Some of the Pharisees in the crowd said to him, Teacher, order your disciples to stop. He answered, I tell you, if these were silent, the stones would shout out.

Jesus Weeps over Jerusalem

As he came near and saw the city, he wept over it, saying, If you, even you, had only recognized on this day the things that make for peace! But now they are hidden from your eyes. Indeed, the days will come upon you, when your enemies will set up ramparts around you and surround you, and hem you in on every side. They will crush you to the ground, you and your children within you, and they will not leave within you one stone upon another; because you did not recognize the time of your visitation from God."

23:44 It was now about noon, and darkness came over the whole land until three in the afternoon, while the sun's light failed; and the curtain of the temple was torn in two. Then Jesus, crying with a loud voice, said, Father, into your hands I commend my spirit. Having said this, he breathed his last.

Luke 19:28-44; 23:44-46

This text from Luke is difficult because it deals with the shadow or the shame that we carry in our own lives.

When Jesus entered Jerusalem, he was entering a high stakes, unresolvable, no-way-out conflict. I mean everybody was locked into their positions. The Jewish people were locked into hating the Romans who for hundreds of years had been oppressing them, undermining the Jews' self-identity as the people of God, chosen to bless all of the world. How could they possibly do that when under the thumb of the Roman Empire? This injustice created in them a spirit of revolt and revolution. But each time a revolt rose up in Israel, the Roman Empire crushed it. There were times when Rome was crucifying five hundred people a day. Jesus was not unusual in that context.

What the Jewish people wanted was the raw power that it would take to turn the tables and overcome the Roman Empire. They knew of the "powerful deeds" that Jesus had done in the countryside so as he came into Jerusalem they cried out, "All hail the King, hallelujah Messiah."

But this king looked at life much differently than they did. If we didn't know that from the earlier chapters of Luke's Gospel, we certainly know it when Jesus weeps over the City of Jerusalem, weeps because even now the people of Jerusalem do not know "the things that make for shalom." Even now after all he'd done and taught they do not understand what it takes to bring about the shalom that God seeks. They cannot see that the raw power to subjugate Rome will simply perpetuate a cycle of violence, a cycle of power, and could not possibly lead towards the blessing and unity this "people of God" was called to offer to the whole world.

Jesus did not want that cycle to continue; he was looking for a shift, an adaptive change. An adaptive change is one that shifts the way people conceive of their positions or relations to one another. He was looking for an adaptive change that would move people beyond an us-versus-them, Roman-versus-Jewish identity. Such an adaptive change requires that people break free of their locked position and so, rather than gather the raw power needed to overcome the Roman occupation, Jesus turned his focus to the Jewish leadership and looked for adaptive change by shifting their identity in the presence of God.

Their religious rituals had turned into a farce, so he walked into the temple and gutted the infrastructure surrounding the sacrificial system. Those laws and rituals were intended to provide a process through which they could examine their own lives and develop and grow. The Torah, the law, was intended to move the people towards shalom, but they used it instead as a way to hide from themselves. They used it to identify themselves as God's pure and righteous people and the Romans as all that was unrighteous, hideous, and evil. Instead of using the laws and rituals to uncover what was breaking them apart and keeping them from shalom, from unity, they used them to hide from the truth and blame Rome for their situation. Were the Romans righteous? Absolutely not. But neither were the people of God, and Jesus knew that for adaptive change to occur and move them to shalom, they had to come to terms with that fact.

But worse than moving them to examine their own lives, Jesus pushed them to re-humanize the Roman people. Jesus simply couldn't work up the self-righteous outrage that a people locked in their position can do. In chapter 13 someone came and told Jesus *about the Galileans whose blood Pilate had mingled with their sacrifices.* The person expected Jesus to be scandalized and outraged at how horribly the righteous, good people of God had been treated, God himself had been blasphemed and the Roman governor was responsible. "Stone him," is what they wanted Jesus to say. But instead Jesus asked them, *Do you think that because these Galileans suffered in this way they were worse sinners than all other Galileans? No, I tell you; but unless you repent, you will all perish as they did.*

"Look within your own heart," he was saying, "find the horror that pollutes your life, and when you turn your eyes on the Romans you will see them in a different light. Instead of investing your energy in hatred, invest your energy in offering them a blessing, for you are called to be a blessing to all the nations of the earth." That's what Jesus was getting at. . . . "Crucify Him," was their response. Now the violence is turned on him. But what's his crime? Simply that he revealed their shame; he showed them just how far they'd wandered from the purposes of God, just how far they were from offering unity and shalom to the world.

Of course they wanted to get rid of him. Their violent anger towards Rome and their violent anger towards Jesus had the same motivation: to do anything to hide the rot and pollution that kept them from the presence of God. Why did they want to hide it? Because looking at one's own failings is painful. If we are to grow towards shalom, towards unity, then we'll have to know the pain of a cross experience by being exposed to our shame. That is the adaptive change that Jesus was looking for and it is exactly what is demanded of us today.

Suppose we were to update the story just a bit. Suppose we were talking about radical Islam and the U.S. Should we view radical Islamists as human beings who come from a particular time and place with their own set of expectations, identities, and wounds, in need of the same love of God as we? Or does it serve our needs better to identify them as evil so that we needn't bother to examine our own lives, the way our nation relates to the rest of the world? We are locked in a cycle of violence. The hard road of adaptive change is the only way to move towards shalom.

Adaptive change is how an evolving creation responds to stress and pain. It's the way the world works. When the current system can no longer be sustained, that is when evolution happens, and it always requires an adaptive change. It is the way it works in cultural and political evolution. It works that way in spiritual evolution. And it works in the physical sphere as well.

I wrote in a previous chapter about Lynn Margulis' groundbreaking work on the first bacterium. There's more to that story and it's quite beautiful. Billions of years ago, at the edges of the sea (evolution happens on the edge), there was a great deal of bacterial life. At some point those bacteria managed to evolve a rudimentary process of photosynthesis. That is, they were able to process light energy into chemical energy and draw upon that to grow and to thrive. In fact they did so well at it that they brought earth's first significant ecological crisis down upon themselves. The byproduct of photosynthesis is of course oxygen and while oxygen is very good for you and me, it is very bad for bacteria. These successful photosynthetic bacteria were literally poisoning themselves with the oxygen they produced. Just as Darwin might have predicted, as the atmosphere became more dense with oxygen, the bacteria began competing for the shrinking resources they needed to survive—for the carbon dioxide. In the end this was a no-way-out situation. It required an adaptive change. Either the bacteria had to change their identity and become a different sort of life form, one that processed energy differently, or they would not survive.

But over time, something surprising and novel began to happen. Margulis showed, and eventually the scientific community agreed, that as the resources became depleted, various bacterial colonies in effect attacked other colonies – they collided. During that process various types of bacteria "took on divisions of labor and donated part of their unique genomes to"[25] a new form of life, the nucleated cell. The bacteria found a way to combine, and together they made the first animal cells—cells that were able to process oxygen. In effect what they did was to give up their individual identities and make an adaptive change in order to evolve.

This process of adaptive change is how individuals evolve and grow and it is how human society evolves as well. When a system is under stress, be it a geo-political crisis, or a neurotic response to what your boss said to you this morning, the conditions for an evolutionary step forward are in place. Of course sometimes the system collapses entirely, sometimes we cannot evolve quickly enough and disaster strikes. If the bacteria hadn't figured out how to use oxygen, then they would not have survived. The reality is, when we are faced with such "stressful moments," there is both opportunity to grow and the danger we will not.

Some time ago one of my seminary students preached a sermon on a passage in Judges. It's such a horrible story I don't even want to tell you where it is. I'm going to tell you just enough of it to make my point, no more. Phyllis Trible,

---

25. Carter Phipps, *Evolutionaries: Unlocking the Spiritual and Cultural Potential of Science' Greatest Idea* (San Francisco: HarperCollins, 2012), 52.

a scholar at Union Seminary in New York, refers to it as a "text of terror," terrifying in particular for its treatment of a woman. It's the story of a Levite who was traveling towards his home with his concubine. He stopped at a city and one of the residents invited him to be a guest at his house. Apparently the men of this city found out that the stranger was there. They came to the door of the house and demanded that the stranger be sent out so they could rape him, use him for their pleasure. Because hospitality is a huge deal in this culture, the owner of the house was therefore honor-bound to protect his Levite guest, and since it was a large crowd, he said to the men, *"Here are my virgin daughter and this man's concubine; let me bring them out now. Ravish them and do whatever you want to them; but against this man do not do such a vile thing."* When they refused, the Levite threw his concubine out the door; she was *"raped and abused all through the night."*

I tell the students in my class to "preach about what God does; find out where God's grace is, and tell us about that."[26] The student who preached the sermon suggested that the grace in the passage comes through raising our ire against the perpetrators of such horrible atrocities. He explained that because such things continue to happen in our world today, this story gives us a focal point to stand against this horror and say, "No more!" I genuinely appreciated his desire to eradicate such unspeakable horror from the world, especially since this student was an unusually empathetic young man. This was not a way to stir up some fervor in the pulpit; no, he himself was disturbed by the horror more deeply than most, I would think. But I was left wondering if our self-righteous ire can provoke the kind of adaptive change that will surely be necessary if we are to eradicate all forms of sexual violence on earth. Can the story do that, or might our self-righteous rage be used to mask something disturbing within our selves?

It is easy to identify ourselves as righteous and good

---

26. Thanks to Elizabeth Achtemeier, Ph.D., my homiletics professor, for inspiring this in me.

when we set our sights on someone guilty of sexual abuse. He—it's usually a he who is the perpetrator of sexual violence—is definitely evil, absolutely wrong, most certainly bad. But there was a young woman in my class who gave us a different kind of view on the issue. What she said was quite beautiful. She had served an internship at a local agency for domestic peace. She trained to work with victims of domestic abuse. She said the training was hard, very hard for her, because she learned that the only way to break the cycle of abuse was to re-humanize the perpetrator. While it may make us feel good, it does nothing to improve the situation if we simply identify the perpetrator as irredeemably bad, an aberrant being to be tossed out with the trash, left with nothing.

We're talking about totally horrifying and unacceptable behavior to be sure. We are talking about a stress point in human relationships, a system that cannot be sustained. It requires an adaptive change, one where the victim no longer identifies herself as worthless, at fault for what happens to her. But we're also talking about creating a situation where the perpetrator is drawn into an environment that invites change, one with clear boundaries on behavior, but one where the darkness and shame in his life can come into the light to be healed. Anything short of that runs the risk of starting the cycle all over again with different partners.[27]

Now it gets personal. We sit in judgment at the Roman's cruel use of power, or we recoil at the spectacle of sexual violence. Our self-righteous ire rises within us as we cast our compassionate eyes on a woman abused by her boyfriend. It is true that all these behaviors are part of a world gone mad, a world that does not know unity, peace, shalom. Certainly our moral judgment should move us to put systems in place that keep such things from happening. But as our self-righteous ire grows within us, something else is going on. If we look

---

27. Please be clear that I am NOT saying that a woman should ever risk her safety by staying in the relationship to "heal it." No, no, no; safety FIRST, then each partner can begin to do the adaptive work that must be done whether they stay together or not.

carefully we will find that we are often covering the polluted shadow living within us. If, metaphorically speaking, we cover the other person with filth, then we look righteous by comparison. Judging the perpetrator is almost a national pastime. A spate of football players is involved in partner abuse so we hear the predictable clarion call. "Somebody should be fired. Let's find out why those bad people do what they do so it will never happen again." I am not saying that what the players or team owners did doesn't matter. It does, and insofar as these incidents shed light on the epidemic of spousal abuse in American society I'm glad it's making the news. But I am also saying that the self-righteous screams of the crowd are hiding something.

When we identify ourselves as "good" and the other as "bad," we are not looking through the eyes of the one who said, "Let there be light," and there was light. We are putting something in shadow. It turns out that God is much less interested in who is "good" and who is "bad," and more interested in seeing each one of us grow and develop.

Every one of us has a unique role to play in the unified whole that is God's creative project. Israel had such a role in the text that prefaces this chapter. They are the people of promise. They are called to reveal the gracious love of God so that all the persons of the earth may receive this blessing. When Jesus approaches Jerusalem he weeps. Sure, he weeps for the people of his heart living under the brutal rule of Rome. But most of all he sees the deep darkness that has covered their hearts. He sees the rage that has caught them up and broken their spirit. He weeps for the blessing lost and waiting to be rediscovered.

All through Luke's story Jesus looks for a way to get the people to examine their shadow, to look at the rage that has grown within them that has caused them to lose sight of who they are as the beloved people of God. Why does he keep bringing them to that place where they have to encounter their shadow? Because it is there in the shadow that they can find the promise and the purpose for which they long.

It is in the shadow that we find our life too. We find our life when we look at whatever we work hard to keep hidden from view. When we expose our shame to the light of day, when we uncover the darkness, we reveal the character of the love that only we can give. We finally crack open what is false and let the joyous expression of God's creative power take hold in the very center of our lives.

That's what the story of Palm Sunday calls us to examine. What leads to unity is neither the alleluia we express when we see someone "get theirs," nor the "crucify him" we shout to deflect attention from our pain. No, the way to unity is the way Jesus shows on his life journey; it is the way that exposes the emptiness of a world separate from the presence of the powerful, creative, evolving love of God.

So look at what you have put in darkness. It will lead you back to the gorgeous life only you can live. That is the way that Jesus chose and it leads to resurrection.

CHAPTER 5

Progress of Meaning

The text that follows isn't a story about Jesus the superman. Matthew's Gospel intends to tell the story of Jesus' life, death, and resurrection so that people can follow him.

> *4:1 Then Jesus was led up by the Spirit into the wilderness to be tempted by the devil. He fasted forty days and forty nights, and afterwards he was famished. The tempter came and said to him, If you are the Son of God, command these stones to become loaves of bread. But he answered, It is written, one does not live by bread alone, but by every word that comes from the mouth of God. Then the devil took him to the holy city and placed him on the pinnacle of the temple, saying to him, If you are the Son of God, throw yourself down; for it is written, He will command his angels concerning you, and On their hands they will bear you up, so that you will not dash your foot against a stone. Jesus said to him, Again it is written, Do not put the Lord your God to the test. Again, the devil took him to a very high mountain and showed him all the kingdoms of the world and their splendor; and he said to him, All these I will give you, if you will fall down and worship me. Jesus said to him, Away with you, Satan! for it is written, Worship the Lord your God, and serve only him. Then the devil left him, and suddenly angels came and waited on him.*
>
> Matthew 4:1-11

This is a wilderness story. The Bible has a rich tradition of wilderness stories. The wilderness is one of those places that holds more and more meaning as the text continues. Hagar and her son Ishmael had their wilderness journey, so did Joseph and David and Elijah and now Jesus. We often think of wilderness as a dusty, hard, dry place, somewhere in the Middle East. But I have been in other kinds of wildernesses. The week between final exams and graduation from high school, my friends Tom, Ted, and I took off for Nova Scotia; we drove all night long up Route One. As I recall we had a little too much fun, but it turned out all right. Once we got to Nova Scotia we parked Ted's old Cougar and went off into the wilderness.

We were initially using paths, but several days later when we realized that we might miss graduation, we decided to leave the paths and instead use our compass to get back to the car. Believe it or not, we didn't get lost. Lost was not the problem. The hemlock forest was the problem. Dense, scratchy forest; it was all we could do to put one foot in front of the other. We came out of it exhausted, tense, dirty, sweaty, scratched and scraped up. Some provisions we thought were important we left along the way.

We'd gotten through that wilderness, and it was a formative experience for us. You know when you're pushed to your limits and you have to let go of everything that's not important? That's the wilderness, that place of formation. Even if it's not a literal wilderness, it's still that place where a spiritual quest happens, a place of challenge.

That's why the story of the people of Israel moving through the wilderness is told. They become formed as the people of God—in the wilderness. Much later, Jesus goes into the wilderness. He goes to be formed as "the Son of God." In each case, when someone goes into the wilderness, they go when their identity has shifted, when who they are or how they see themselves changes.

Of course the primary wilderness story in the Bible is that of the Exodus. God's people were enslaved in Egypt.

God saved God's people by bringing them out of Egypt, out of the land of slavery. They were no longer slaves; they were free. They were shifting identity. The transition from slavery to freedom takes a lifetime. In the case of the Israelites, an entire generation lived and died before they were ready to be God's people and move into the Promised Land. These wilderness stories taken as a whole tell us about what it takes to be free. It's in the wilderness where these things are worked out, where we are formed into the people of God, where we figure out what to do with the change that has taken place in us.

The Spirit drove Jesus into the wilderness just as he was responding to a clarion call from the heavens, *"This is my Son, the Beloved."* Jesus was being called to be the one who's responsible for the Kingdom of God.

The setting of the story is an agricultural society. In any agricultural society it is the oldest son, his character and his wisdom, that determine the texture and the character of the estate. In this case, Jesus, the "eldest son" reflects the character of the Kingdom of God. This is why the King of Israel is referred to as "God's son" in the Hebrew Scriptures.[28] It may seem an odd comparison, but consider all of Jane Austen's novels—*Pride and Prejudice, Mansfield Park, Emma*. At one level they may each seem like a simple romantic intrigue; traditionally men turn up their collective nose at such things. But there is much more to Austen than that. Each one of those novels is about the character of the sons who will inherit the estate in an agricultural society. If the one to inherit is someone of good character, then the entire estate will thrive—not just the owner and his family but the surrounding villages and farms as well. It's all about the eldest son.

From the moment Jesus is identified as God's son, he moves into the wilderness to be formed for the journey ahead. Some think these temptations are about Jesus being tested, as though he might pass or fail the test. But it's not that kind of test. It's the kind of test that forms someone's character.

---

28. For instance: Psalm 2:7.

There's no worry about whether or not he's going to fail the test or succeed at it. Rather, he has to go through the experience to grow into the person God is calling him to be. That's the kind of test this was. Jesus' character needed to be set in place in order to do the work of the Son of God.

Scholars compare these two wilderness stories of Jesus and the Israelites. There are echoes of the Exodus in this story about Jesus. Each one of these temptations in Matthew involves a quotation from Deuteronomy. Deuteronomy tells the story of the Exodus from beginning to end. Each of these quotations is taken from a story about when the people of Israel failed one test or another. It is easy to think that the point of Jesus' story is that he got it right where the Israelites got it wrong, but let's not be lulled into accepting only that simple interpretation.

The fundamental issue of moving from slavery to freedom remains in each story. That's the beauty of the Exodus story. As with other Scripture, when we engage it, the text allows for interpretation and reflection on the nature of freedom from different perspectives. Matthew takes the story in a fresh direction.

Let's take the stones-turned-to-bread temptation. This comes from a time in the Exodus story when the people were complaining. God had saved them, brought them out of the land of Egypt, out of the house of bondage, and as they moved into the wilderness there wasn't enough food to eat and they started complaining to Moses. "Oh, you just brought us out here to die." They had absolutely no trust in the movement and power of God—even after all God had done for them. Their story is about learning to trust God to provide.

That's not exactly the same thing Jesus was dealing with—at least not on the same level. Jesus was tempted to misuse power. It wasn't about trusting God to fill his perceived needs. For Jesus, it was about trusting God's plan and creative purpose for his life. This story assumes that Jesus had the power to turn stones into bread. He could use his own power to fill his own needs. The question was what kind of an impact would that have on the world around him? The question is: will he use his power to serve himself, or will he use it to further the way and purpose of the creative Word of God? Jesus chose the higher consciousness, Jesus stood where he could see what God was about in the created order. He sought to further God's work, so he said, "No." No, human beings don't live by bread alone. No, it's not simply about having my needs met; real freedom is about something more. It involves trust in the creative word that goes forth and makes beauty out of chaos. Trust forms freedom within.

Next the Devil brings Jesus to the pinnacle of the temple and tells him to jump off. "Don't worry, the angels will save you; it says so in the good book . . . really." In response Jesus refers to an incident when the Israelites were in the wilderness at Meribah. In that situation the Israelites didn't have water. God's given them food, God's rescued them from Egypt, God's been faithful to them, but they're scared there's not enough water. So once again they complain to Moses: "Take us back to Egypt. We'd rather go back into slavery than die of thirst out here." Again, they're learning how to trust, learning whether or not God will give what's needed.

But this second time around, their response raises a question for me, "What would it take for them to trust God? What would it take for them to trust that God was going to take care of them?" Or maybe more to the point—never mind them, let's ask ourselves—"If God were a wish-fulfillment machine, if God could fill all your wishes, what would God have to do to get you to trust that God would care for and love you? (I know what it would take for me. It's pretty neurotic. The way I was brought up saddled me with a psychological dilemma that some preachers' kids deal with. I was in competition with Jesus for my parents' time and love. Jesus was the overachieving older brother in my life. What would God need to do to convince me that God loves me? I'd literally have to start a new religion . . . and it would have to be pretty darn successful too, otherwise my small, neurotic self can't trust that God's power is unfolding within me, loving me in the same way as Jesus. Crazy I know and I hope I've grown beyond that.) But when we get down to that place of fear, wondering whether or not God is going to take care of us, whether or not the universe can be trusted to fill our perceived needs, what would it take to make you trust God?

That is the question that comes to Jesus. The Devil's challenging him: Find out whether or not you can trust. But Jesus wasn't going there. Jesus knew that he would be jumping into the abyss soon enough. He was learning to trust God at the moment when life is forfeit. He wasn't even looking to God to save his life at that moment. His consciousness was bigger: he took a step up in consciousness, saw the entire sweep of God's creative project, and sought his own place within it. He wasn't going to jump off to serve his own neurotic need, but he was preparing to jump at a moment that would give life meaning. He would jump in the context of God's creative project. He did that the moment he faced the cross several years later in Jerusalem. Trusting, even at the moment when life is forfeit, is what forms freedom within.

The third temptation is about idolatry—trusting in things that allow you to control creation. "Bow down to me and I'll give you all the power the world can muster," is essentially what the Devil was saying to Jesus. It's more tempting than you might think. What would you decide? The Devil says, "I'll give you all the power you could possibly need to get the things done the way you want to get things done. Think about it . . . You could right so many wrongs. You'd get your way. I'll give you everything you need to be able to pull it off." What would you do?

Jesus had an agenda; he actually thought there should be a just society. He thought that poor people should have what they needed in order to survive and thrive. He thought kindness and compassion should be operating in the world, not war and death. The Devil offered him the power to make that happen and Jesus turned it down. Why? The question gets at two different views of power. One way to define power is the ability to make people do what they do not want to do.

Progress of Meaning

By whatever force available to you, power is the ability to construct a world of your liking. The other kind of power is creative power, the Word or Logos. This power trusts in the evolutionary moves of creation from death to surprising new life. Trusting in one leads to slavery, trusting in the other leads to freedom.

Idolatry is about grasping hold of the power that constructs a world of our liking. The Israelites who first lived with these stories as Scripture were a practical lot, which is to say they were human and smart. If your crops weren't doing well and your neighbor, two tribes over said, "We worship this other god and our crops are doing fine," it's going to be really tempting to pray to this new god, especially if you don't understand weather patterns, or soil conditions, or whatever else goes into growing crops.

But it's about more than magically controlling crops. This issue of coercive power and how to use it shows up in any number of arenas. For the followers of Jesus in Matthew's time it showed up big time in the economic arena, which strangely had a lot to do with whether or not they would bow down to Caesar.

During Roman occupation people were pretty much allowed to worship whatever god they wanted just so long as they also worshiped Caesar. In fact, Caesar's cult, that is the religious institution that was built around emperor worship, was also integrally involved in the banking system, the transfer of money and property. So if Jews did not want to "bow down to Caesar," they were facing a life on the outside economically. It would have been a little like living in the U.S. without a credit card. They couldn't participate in the economic structures of the time in order to get ahead if they did not bow down to Caesar. There was a real temptation to go ahead and use those unjust structures to make a world that fit their vision of what's right and what's wrong.

That's the temptation: Are you going to live by the power to construct the world as you would like it, or are you going to trust the creative word of God, which is the expression of

God's love for all creation? Jesus said, "No, I'm not going to grasp hold of that kind of coercive power. I'm going to trust in the nature of God's creative power. I'm going to trust in the power of God that brings new life out of the ashes."

This question of whether we're willing to use coercive power is a difficult question to be sure and it takes us to a challenging place. There is a lot going on in the world that is very, very bad. If we have the coercive power to change it, to construct a more just world, then aren't we morally obligated to do so? This is the question we Americans ask when we see a dictator torturing and killing people at will within the borders of another nation. We have the weapons, we have the power to stop such atrocities: should we intervene? We wonder just how far we should go in using the coercive power at our disposal to construct a just society. It's a question without simple answers, but the text is clear enough: if we are relying on coercive power to construct the world as we would want it, then freedom, and I would add, justice, will elude us.

Intuitively we know this, for we know that violence begets violence. The key here is to rely on and act in concert with the creative love-power of God in the world, and that is tricky business indeed, for can we trust ourselves to figure out what that is? It requires discernment and a healthy skepticism about our own ability to forego the use of the power within our grasp.

On the one hand, we can say, "Everything is wrong; it's awful and I have to fix it." From that space it is our ego, our power that is being exercised to satisfy our desires—however high-minded we might think them to be. This is how our false self embraces power in an effort to construct a secure scenario within which to live life. That is what Jesus would call "bowing down to Caesar." That is what Jesus rejected.

But there is another approach, a trusting approach that forms you and frees you when you live connected to the source, and that is the creative love that powers creation. It sounds outrageous. It even can sound downright wrong until you look beneath the surface. In communion with the source that loves creation into being, instead of saying, "Everything is wrong and I have to fix it," we say, "In this moment, everything is as it should be; not that everything is complete and perfect, but everything is as it should be in this moment that God is creating. There are next steps to be sure, but in this moment, I can trust the creative process, I can trust God for the unfolding of creation." I do not rely on my false self to construct reality.

It is a very different place from which to act, for the false images of the self have been cleared away. The "I am x, y and z..." *because* my parents met so many years ago, *because* I had this experience, or that lover, or made that mistake, *because* I live with this shame, or this set of talents, or this set of wounds, of with this excess income at my disposal—all that is cleared away. When we simply act from our I AM, with no qualifiers as Dr. King said in an earlier chapter, then we are free, free to express the love of God that is uniquely ours to express. We are free of the fear and hopelessness generated by our false self, a false self disconnected from creative source and unable to effect real change. That is the very definition of freedom.

It's hard, but Jesus calls us precisely to this different kind of trust. This story about Jesus' temptation in the wilderness asks us to become disciples, to follow Jesus rather than take hold of the power that will adjust the world in ways that we judge it ought to be. Everything is as it should be right in this moment. But everything is dynamic and will change, because the power of God is evolving and making all things new.

The question is can we trust that things will work out? Is that reasonable in an outrageously painful and horrifying world? These are grasping questions, questions that seek control rather than the creative love of God. It is only the God who has brought us to this moment, only the God whose heart we know and whose tears we know, who can give us freedom and bring the next moment into being.

The stories of Scripture point the way as we grow into trusting God ever more profoundly. We learn to trust as consciousness develops and our understanding of humanity's place in the Kosmos evolves. We come to know that it's not about me: it's about the power of all creation. It's about the unity of which each one of us is a part.

It's that unity that we serve; in fact it can't be achieved unless you show up. God can't get it done without you. You have a unique role to play in trusting the powerful creative Spirit to unfold within you. Joy and freedom are ours when we live our lives in the creative arms of God.

So in the quiet, let these questions and temptations form you. What would it take, what would God need to do for you, to make you trust the universe as it unfolds? What's important to you? What gives your life meaning? Jesus is calling you to follow him. Will you live as long as you can as comfortably as you can, or will you open your lives to that larger, truer reality, that gorgeous project we call God's creation?

PART II

THEOLOGICAL QUESTIONS FOR EVOLUTIONARY CHRISTIANS

(word cloud featuring: God, world, nature, Christian, becoming, about, around, conversation, another, something, human, way, put, people, second, most, Jesus, cross, face, believe, understanding, much, called, place, time, own, sacrifice, presence, new, sense, make, work, just, whole, violence, story, being, things, only, life, prayer, end, while, take, little, pray, back, power, Scriptures, like, sin, Bible, going, tribes, true, made, each, first, faith, say, between, thing, truth, day, three, really, creation, years, live, relationship, God's, come, over, unique, love, gave, understand, know, person, Spirit, some, tradition, want, Divine, creative, Trinity, always, all, whether, because, purpose, created, other, traditions, think, more, said, one, see, within)

The Christian tradition has been under fire for some time now. When was the last time you saw more than a one-dimensional representation of a Christian in the media? Usually it's of a priest offering a sanctimonious prayer to open a political meeting, or maybe that whole ashes to ashes, dust to dust thing at a funeral.

I think there are some good reasons for this state of affairs. We in the church have lost track of the message of grace, letting it be drowned out by words of judgment and fear or archaic words that modern people simply do not understand. In short, we sound silly.

But if we toss the faith story out, if we simply deconstruct our traditional religious structures and do not reconstruct something true from within them, we will have lost a truth that is not easily found. The Hebrew people had an astonishing spiritual intuition. They described it and shared it in the only way they knew how – from within their own worldview. When that message met the Greco-Roman world, it was described anew from within another thought world. We call that Christianity. The message we call gospel is always shared and interpreted from within the thought world of the one who seeks to know God.

My challenge then is to understand what those ancient peoples were pointing at as they developed the major theological motifs—the Trinity or atonement or God's answers to prayer. These are ideas that, at least in their native form, don't make much sense to the modern mind. But if I'm going to be faithful to the tradition and look for the love, the hope, and the freedom of gospel, rather than tossing the book away, then I have to wrestle with those strange theological motifs. That's what I'm doing in this next section of the book. But I'm trying to do more than that: I want to suggest to you why these things matter, why it makes a difference in your life to understand and live with them.

CHAPTER 6

Why Preach on the Bible in the Twenty-first Century?

What are the Scriptures and why would anyone pay any attention to them? Do the Hebrew and Christian texts hold any exclusive claim on the truth? Those are legitimate questions in a modern world. After all, at first blush the Bible offers a vision of God that runs completely contrary to scientific observation. Just think of that verse in the Noah story, the story of the forty-day Flood, in Genesis, where the text says, "God remembered Noah and all the wild animals . . . and God made a wind blow over the earth, and the waters subsided; the fountains of the deep *and the windows of the heavens were closed*," (Genesis 8:1-2). This author thinks that the earth is flat, that there is a dome above the earth, and that above that dome, there is water (which is apparently why the sky is blue!) So if God wants to make it rain, then all He, (for the author, God is "He") has to do is open the windows of heaven. When He wants it to stop, He shuts the windows of heaven. We know that is not true, so why listen to these stories?

And why listen to stories whose implications are far worse than whether or not God closes heavenly windows to stop and start rainfall—stories about horrendous violence, for example, that for centuries have been used to justify horrifying acts of violence. Why should we listen to them? Of course people who hold to a traditional-mythic worldview would say we listen to them because God dictated them to inspired authors so we ignore them at our peril. Well, that's one approach, but it's obviously not mine. I'm willing to transcend the traditional-mythic point of view and accept common sense and the findings of modern criticism.

Yes, the story of how the Scriptures came into being is beautifully long and complex. Scholars have determined, for instance, that there are four major layers of editing extant in the Torah, the first five books of the Hebrew Scriptures. In response to the attacks of the Philistines on Palestine, first King Saul and then eventually King David were able to consolidate a group of twelve tribes into the nation of Israel. Over time this coalition of tribes, not having blood ties to hold them together, began the work of weaving together a tapestry of their reflections on the nature of God, their purpose and obligation in the world. They wove them into a narrative that gave them an identity, gave them some sense of their purpose in the world. And so this story is told of Abram, the progenitor of all twelve tribes:

> *12:1 Now the Lord said to Abram, Go from your country and your kindred and your fathers house to the land that I will show you. 2 I will make of you a great nation, and I will bless you, and make your name great, so that you will be a blessing. 3 I will bless those who bless you, and the one who curses you I will curse; and in you all the families of the earth shall be blessed*
>
> Genesis 12:1-3

This coalition of tribes understood that God's purpose was to bless all the families of the earth and that their obligation and call was to be the agents or conduits of that blessing. We can argue about whether they accomplished that purpose, but that was their self-understanding and the narrative they developed in Scripture gave texture to that vision.

But the story didn't end there. Following the death of David's son, Solomon, the twelve tribes were unable to stay together. The two southern tribes, headquartered in Jerusalem, and the ten northern tribes, split. In response to this, the northern tribes began editing the stories of the Torah. They put their own particular cast on the understanding of this God of blessing. We call this editor the "Elohist" because this author refers to the Divine as "Elohim." (Interestingly, "Gods" in the plural.) The history of these twelve tribes and their interactions continued until 722 BCE, when the first Empire power to rise on earth, Assyria, came south and in a brutal war wiped the ten northern tribes from the face of the earth.

I am over-simplifying here, but the response of the two southern tribes was to enter a period of renewal. To them it was clear that the north had been destroyed because they had not been faithful to the God who sought to bless all the families of the earth. The renewal movement produced the third editor who even added yet another document to Torah, Deuteronomy. The "Deuteronomist," as this editor is called, edited the narratives of both the northern and southern tribes and in so doing gave the stories his own particular understanding of God and of the people's obligation to God and the world.

Eventually the Assyrian Empire was defeated and the Babylonian Empire rose to take its place. In 587 BCE, the Babylonians besieged Jerusalem, defeated the southern tribes, and exiled the entire ruling class to Babylon. This historical reality had a profound effect on the Israelites and while they were in exile their priests gathered them into community and began to develop an understanding of what happened. When the Persian Empire rose up over the Babylonians and sent the Israelite exiles home to Jerusalem, the Israelites rebuilt their Temple and restarted their religious traditions. As part of that restoration, the Priestly writers produced the final edit of Torah. Interestingly, it was only then that the first chapter of Genesis—the "six day creation" poem—was added.

Throughout all of this time, throughout the rises and the falls of fortune, people were writing and commenting on this Torah. Prophets like Amos spoke to the northern tribes, prophets like Jeremiah to the south. The Book of Isaiah alone seems to have been edited over a period of four hundred years as people sought to understand God's relationship to this new kind of power – empire power – on the earth. Writers like the poet of Song of Songs and the preacher of Ecclesiastes all commented on Torah during particular historical circumstances from within particular worldviews.

What we call the New Testament, or the Christian Scripture, also comments on this same Torah. The authors of the New Testament were fundamentally Jewish writers, seeking to understand Torah. In what is one of the great tragedies of history their interpretation of Torah was so different from the mainstream that what had been a Jewish sect, Christianity, split from the source religion of its primary text, Torah.

At various times groups of people canonized some of these reflections on Torah. That is, they made them normative for the community's conversation. Torah was canonized first, then the Prophets, and finally the Writings which completed the three parts of the Hebrew canon. Then finally Christians gathered and made the documents of what are traditionally called the New Testament normative for their conversation. That's what the Bible is: a set of documents representative of thousands of years of reflection concerning the nature of God and our obligation and purpose on this earth.

For 2,000 years now theologians, philosophers, preachers, priests—anyone who can read—have continued the conversation about these Scriptures. Groupings of these Scriptures seed the conversation we have today as Christians and as Jews and as Muslims. So when I stand up in the pulpit, what I offer is the next word in that thousands-of-years-long conversation, a conversation that began with tribes telling stories around the campfire and morphed over centuries of history as layer after layer of editing evolved them further. I'm offering the next word in that same conversation and I expect others—like you—to provide the word after that. I relish the opportunity because I believe the conversation grounded in these Scriptures reveals a creation that is driven forward by the creative presence of a God who seeks only blessing, only beauty.

That's what I think the Scriptures are and why I care about them. But that raises the question: are the Hebrew and Christian scriptures the only ones that can seed a conversation about the nature of God and our purpose and obligation in this world?

Short Answer: Absolutely Not.

Longer Answer: In the same way that I assume the Spirit of God has unfolded this process of revelation within the Hebrew and Christian texts, I also believe the same Spirit reveals the nature of God in other ways and at other times in human history. What I've said about the Hebrew and Christian scriptures specifically can also be said about sacred texts generally around the globe. As a religious tradition evolves and grows, sacred texts reflecting those traditions develop around them. The traditions that derive from Torah—Judaism, Islam, Christianity, Mormonism and so forth—-are text-centric traditions. Other traditions, among them the Native American religious traditions, are less text focused. This doesn't mean that their texts are of less value, only that that community does not see them in quite the same way, as normative for their faith, as we do ours. In short, sacred texts form and inform traditions. Since I don't think that Christianity has a corner on the truth, I do look at other religions and texts with interest and respect. But this is different than accepting them as equally normative for me. This moves to what an Integral view of Christianity is.

An Integral view accepts the insights of modernism, specifically its deconstruction of myths, and recognizes they are not literally true. So an Integral view can be said to "transcend" the traditional-mythic stage of development. In so doing, most pure modernists sit in judgment over the texts. Once deconstructed, the texts become artifacts of a bygone era with little practical use for today.

I think we lose something important when we write off the scriptures in that way. I think that the ancients' experience of the Divine is every bit as valid as yours or mine—maybe more so. (They were after all, more attuned to state experiences than we are.) To be sure they described those experiences from within their own worldview, in the only way they knew how, through their myths. But I am interested in the encounter they had with God. I am interested in understanding what they are pointing towards with their myths. I want to understand those experiential realties from within my own worldview. And so while I go beyond understanding the texts literally, I nevertheless value the insights gleaned from the conversation with them. So while I transcend their mythic frame, I very definitely include them in the formation of my faith. In fact they are normative for my understanding of God and God's interaction with creation.

Similarly an Integral view of Christianity accepts the insights of the pluralist worldview. It recognizes that all truth necessarily derives from a perspective and that no single perspective can lay claim to exclusive truth. The pluralist can be said to transcend the literal claim on truth the biblical authors make. That said, I've found that most pure pluralists move from that idea to an attitude that it does not matter what you believe, and so the pluralist often – not always, but often—finds herself pulling together a pastiche of religious perspectives that suits her current needs. I believe she does so at her peril. For that reason I claim the Christian tradition as my own; I submit myself to its authority and embrace the challenge of understanding it in my own context. But that is tricky, for my way is not the only way a faithful person can integrate both the modern and the pluralist critique with integrity. I want to keep the insights of the traditional mythic frame because I believe that I need a tradition to hold me accountable, to challenge me, but others feel called to develop a new tradition out of the depth structures of the existing traditions.

If religions are like languages, then I imagine that in several thousand years there will be one universal language; there may be dialects, but the universal language will have evolved as our society becomes ever closer to one another in communication. I assume that such will be the case with religions. I think those who are developing what we call a "trans-lineage path" are pioneers. I am not one, but I'm very interested in engaging with them in dialogue. Why? Because I would like the "grammar" of Christianity to be part of this new trans-lineage religious language and because I want to understand the depth structures of the other traditions. But most important, I believe that through that conversation I am called to renewal in my own tradition.

Not too long ago I spent a week with people from a whole variety of faiths and traditions—500 people, from 33 countries and 6 continents. The Rabbis were very Jewish, the Swamis very Hindu, the Senseis very Buddhist, the Priests and Ministers (including me), very Christian. Being together encouraged none of us to leave our own tradition. Being together moved all of us to a deeper place within our own faith, the kind of place that promotes real development and change, the kind of place where connection to that certain something we call God makes it possible to move beyond our limited imaginations to a new creation, the kind of place that can make the difference between our destruction and our evolution.

This is what I call an Integral approach to Christian faith. I seek to be faithful to the Hebrew and Christian Scriptures, I seek to be formed from within the Christian tradition, but I do so while actively engaging with people in other traditions and those who seek a trans-lineage tradition. So while this book is about viewing evolutionary faith in the Christian tradition, it does not claim that Christians have an exclusive hold on the truth.

CHAPTER 7

Making Sense of the Cross?

An earlier chapter blithely refers to the cross and resurrection as being at the heart of Christian faith. That is problematic to say the least. We should take care not to let such a poetic phrase obscure the horrifying truth to which it refers. For it has been used over and over again to set the context for violence. It is a violent metaphor.

Religion, philosopher Rene Girard believes, was invented at least in part to curb violence and so it was that systems of sacrifice were developed as a means to transfer violence away from people and onto animals. The problem of course is that this does not break the cycle of violence itself. In fact, by assuming the cycle of violence, sacrifice actually justifies it. This is the single biggest objection I have to the motif of cross and resurrection—of sacrifice as a means to receive righteousness—and it's a whopper. I'm with my friend Carren on this, "We ought to take all those big Ts down from the wall in the front of the sanctuary and put up a big baby instead."

On the other hand, frustrating though it may be, as I explained in the last chapter, I'm also responsible to my tradition[29] so I can't just toss it out. But the search to understand has borne some fruit for there are other ways to look at this motif. In fact this violent metaphor of sacrifice wasn't even the dominant theory of atonement for the first thousand years of Christian history. It only gained real traction in the work

---

29. That's important to me. If I simply put together a pastiche of beliefs that fit my sensibilities I'll never be challenged to grow, never be driven towards transformation. It's why I still call myself a Christian. Others, (like my wife), seem quite able to do so, but that is not my path—at least not so far.

of Anselm, a theologian during the eleventh century.

Historically there have been three main atonement theories. For a thousand years the "Christus Victor" theory of atonement held sway. It spiritualizes the cross event. It says that when Jesus was crucified, he descended into hell, the place of devils and evil spirits, and there Jesus defeated the powers of evil so that they no longer have power over those who trust in Christ's spiritual power. In defeating the evil spiritual powers, Christ defeats death – evil's weapon—and is resurrected to new life.[30]

The second major theory is what most people consider to be the only atonement theory today—substitutionary atonement. In its simple form it goes something like this. Here's the problem: you are very, very, bad, hopelessly bad, depraved, worthless. God on the other hand is perfect and holy and cannot abide the presence of evil. Therefore God must punish the evildoer if the evil doer (you) is to come into God's presence. The trouble is that the punishment is eternal damnation, death. But, so the story goes, God loves you sooooo much that God sent his Son Jesus to die a horrible, tortuous death on a cross instead of you. So now, all you have to do is believe that God did this wonderful thing for you and you will find yourself on the right side of God's naughty and nice list; you'll go to heaven.

You see the problem: God may love you, but you have to wonder about a God who can only be satisfied by the shedding of blood – anyone's blood. It made more sense when we thought that blood had magical properties, but we don't think that anymore, so I think we can do without this theory, period.

The third theory is called moral influence. In this theory, Jesus is seen as faithful to the end. He is true to his mission, true to God, true to humanity. He loves perfectly, caring for

---

30. Remember now, they were writing from within their own worldview, not ours. I'll not go into it here, but the dharma question that arises is, "Why did they describe Christ's death in that way and no some other way? How am I to understand the spiritual experience that drove their interpretation?"

all, including his captors, the religious leaders, and his executioners who, let's be clear, were not the Jews, but the Roman soldiers. Jesus is so true to his calling to express the perfect love of God that when we see him on the cross we recognize our own complicity in the horror of the world, and are moved to follow him, loving as he loved. There is something to this theory—unless we pervert it to say that there is a God out there who decided to kill his Son so we would be inspired to follow him.

There are other atonement theories—twenty-seven in the Christian scriptures alone, I'm told. There is one in particular that is useful for an evolutionary view of Christian faith. It comes at the end of the Gospel of John. Jesus is on the cross and the Roman soldiers stick a spear in his side to make sure he is dead. Out comes blood and water. The Gospel of John is a self-consciously symbolic Gospel. By the time we have reached this point in the story, we already know that the blood that pours out of his side symbolizes his life, or life force. The water that pours out symbolizes the Spirit of this enfleshed creative power of God. So in John's Gospel, where the climax of the story is the death and not the resurrection, it is actually when Jesus dies that his life force and his Spirit pour out into the world, and new life and a powerful creative Spirit are set loose in creation. In other words, in death (anyone's death, the enfleshed logos is paradigmatic of all humanity) life and Spirit pour into creation and seed the next transformational step of evolution.

There is a similar point made at the end of the Gospel of Luke. In Luke's story Jesus is on the cross. He is mocked and told he should get himself off the cross. But he chooses instead to remain and as he dies he says, "Father into your hands I commend my Spirit," as if to say that in death his Spirit, his creative loving Spirit is set loose in creation to drive the next beautiful move of creation forward.

It is these atonement theories I point to when I say that cross and resurrection reflect the evolutionary nature of creation. The ancient writers were describing their sense of the nature of God and God's interaction with creation in the only way they knew how, from within their own mythic worldview. As we seek the dharma, our work is to ask what the interaction was, so that we can describe it from within our own worldview.

So I'm done with substitutionary atonement. I'm done with the magical notion that human beings need to sacrifice in order to appease an angry God. It causes too much damage.

Sixteen people died at the hands of Sgt. Bales the week before I wrote this. You can probably call to mind some equally horrifying moment in our recent history as you read. Sixteen innocent Afghanis dead. It's not entirely clear what happened, but one thing we can say: life had betrayed Sgt. Bales. Something had gone terribly awry, rage overwhelmed the moment, and erupted in a horrifying act of violence.

René Girard refers to this as mimetic violence, violence that erupts when life has betrayed us, when we've not received our due, as though there is some standard against which our life is measured. But no such ideal exists. In its place is an endless spiral of comparisons and envy, a spiral that leaves us paralyzed by shame. We think we are less than, one down to someone's one up. Then realizing we do not measure up, like Cain,[31] the rage builds within us until it erupts on the nearest victim. It happened in Afghanistan that week. It happens to one in four married women, each bearing her husband's rage on her body. It happens when a community discovers some weakness in a person whose life was thought to have measured above our own—a spiritual teacher, a celebrity. The vitriolic web attacks that tear into the reputations of those who have indeed fallen short are a response to our shame, not theirs. And so the cycle of mimetic violence continues its downward spiral.

Societies have used a variety of strategies to protect themselves from such violence. The ancients did so by putting a sacrificial system in place. All shame, guilt, rage, and hatred

---

31. Genesis 4.

were poured into the sacrifice and drained of their power, destroyed in the altar fires or exiled into the wilderness. This was no peaceful ritual done as the congregation engaged in centering prayer.

That sacrificial metaphor remains too active today, distorting our understanding of God. It was certainly part of my spiritual formation. "Put that on the cross with Jesus, Sam," Mrs. Mac would say. By "that," she invariably meant some natural expression of adolescence.

It is enough that these ritual acts of violence live on in our minds and ultimately support the downward spiral of mimetic violence. Suggesting that the cross is an effective way to appease an angry God for all the horror that characterizes the human species is not only magical thinking but dangerous thinking.

Let's be clear: Jesus was indeed sacrificed on the cross, but it was *not* something God required. Like the sacrifice Cain offered, it was offered without God's command. Like the sacrifice Cain offered, the sacrifice of Jesus on the cross was made only to assuage our fear, to excise our shame. Further, when humanity sacrificed Jesus, God answered with a resounding, "No. I will not have it. I'll turn your sacrifice on its head." And so God raised Jesus from the dead. (Whether one understands this in a literal fashion or as a metaphor in the context of story is of little consequence to me as I make this particular point.)

God rejects the cycle of mimetic violence and offers new life to those who bear the weight of injustice in the world. That is the biblical story. Liberation theologians rightly describe it as "God's preferential option for the poor," the Prophets spoke for the orphan and the widow, Christ sought justice in a world overwhelmed by tyranny: *This* is God's nature.

But it is not only the victims who are healed by the creative love of God. Sacrifice that appeases an angry God does not exhaust the metaphor. Much of sacrifice is focused on restoring community. Consider that the texts concerning sacrifice sound like preparations for a large wild party.[32] We don't often think of it that way, if we think about what sacrifice was like at all. But it is a community forming moment. Sacrifice and community gathering go hand in hand. The person bringing a sacrifice to the altar has recognized his responsibility for defacing the beauty of human communion in the presence of God. He then takes the next step; he brings the sacrifice as a first step towards community restoration. He's bringing food for the party. That is an entirely different way to view sacrifice, is it not? Looking at the sacrifice of Jesus on the cross in this way, a much different picture emerges.

We often ask, "How can a good God, a God of love and compassion allow the violence and injustice of this world to stand? Where was God when Sgt. Bales walked off the base to commit this atrocity? Think about it: aren't we talking about the fundamental betrayal? Doesn't the injustice we experience, life's betrayal as it were, metaphorically fall back on the hand that guides creation? What is God's answer?

Let's open our minds to this: God offers a sacrifice as a first step towards community restoration. It is as though God recognizes God's complicity in the cycle of violence and takes responsibility for a creation where justice has yet to prevail. God offers a self-sacrifice as a way to create the beauty of human communion in the presence of God's creative love.[33]

We don't understand what mechanism the ancients thought was at work, but we do know they thought of Christ's sacrifice as offering a restored life, a new life capable of reversing the cycle of mimetic violence. It is why the sacrifice of Jesus was to be "once for all" (Hebrews 10:2).

If we look at the sacrifice this way, "following Jesus" means we are called to examine our lives, take responsibility for our complicity in the cycle of violence defacing creation,

---

32. Read Leviticus 1 and I think you'll see what I mean.
33. I'm grateful to Dr. Annette Schellenberg, Dr. Annette Weissenrieder, Dr. James Noel, and especially Dr. Gregory Love for their input at a symposium sponsored by San Francisco Theological Seminary as I worked out these ideas. By this I do not mean to imply that their views are in line with mine.

and take steps towards healing the fracture. We need to "bring food to the party." For then, empowered by the new life given by God, we will turn the spiral of violence upside down. The rage will drain out of this human community and we will move ever closer towards a world formed in the creative love of God.

CHAPTER 8

Trinity and the Three Faces of Spirit

It is said that there is one God who is known in three persons, each individuated person being the entirety of God. It doesn't make sense, but there it is: the Doctrine of the Trinity in a nutshell. Since 325 CE, the Church has said, "If it isn't Trinitarian, then it isn't Christian." It is debatable whether or not the early church councils were correct in their formulation, but for the purpose of this essay we'll take it as an historical fact: if it isn't Trinitarian, it isn't Christian . . . which is curious because we Christians pretty much ignore the Trinity. Really, apart from giving it lip service and a few pretty cool hymns Christians, especially over the last century or two, have pretty much ignored the doctrine. That's not too surprising; after all, it doesn't really make any sense.

People long ago developed the notion of the Trinity to answer their questions, questions that we do not share. Modernists really don't believe that there is a "Father God" out there somewhere who had a "Son," and so we don't really care whether the Father and the Son are of the same substance or not. That was a big deal in 325 CE, but now it seems like an arcane notion that has little to do with a context of meaning in which we live our lives.

Initially however, the doctrine of the Trinity had a great deal to do with the context of meaning in which people lived their lives. The question is, as modernism has deconstructed the myth or even the being of the Trinitarian God, is there anything left? Does the Trinitarian God have any relevance in our world?

The people who debated and fought over the doctrine of the Trinity were trying to understand the circumstances of their own lives in relationship to the creator, to its ebbs and flows, to its brutality and its beauty. They were trying to understand this within the living tradition of Judaism.

They knew on the one hand that they experienced God in three ways, and yet they also had some deep intuition that there was but one God, so they formulated the doctrine of the Trinity, a doctrine that was never logically coherent. That's probably a good thing, since if I told you I had a logically coherent definition of God, I'd either be missing something or lying. We are talking about the God "about whom naught can be said."[34] Words, ideas, even intuitions fail us, for the mystery of God lives beyond the limits of knowledge.

For all of that, we still try and pierce the mystery, because we are called to the struggle with core issues of faith like what it means to be free. We struggle with the relationship between our behavior and the suffering we endure. We want to know why we're here and what we're about. We too, long for connection with the Divine. Such struggles are built into the fabric of humanity. Archaeologists and anthropologists tell us that from the moment humans became human, and maybe before, we've been religious creatures, that is, creatures who seek to understand their origins, to know their maker, and to understand the power that drives creation, its direction and purpose. We want to know God.

It is possible that all our musings about God are simply humanity's desires and dreams "writ large across the cosmos."[35] While I cannot deny that as a theoretical possibility, and certainly that is in part what is going on, nevertheless for me a purposeless creation doesn't make sense of the fact that in 13.82 billion years creation has evolved from the Big Bang to Shakespeare.

What fascinates me is that while our ideas about God and our answers to the fundamental questions about pur-

---

34. Attributed to Alice Bailey.
35. Attributed to Ludwig Feuerbach.

pose and creative power have evolved just as everything else evolves, it is also true that all over the globe, no matter our stage of development, humans seem to point in the same directions when describing their experience of the Divine.

There was a time when humanity existed in small, nomadic, hunter-gatherer tribes. These wandering tribes, held together by blood ties, saw the mysteries of creation—flooding rains, dry deserts, exploding mountains—and determined that gods, spirits, and demons were controlling their destinies. So they sought to know their gods, they tried to understand how their gods controlled creation. They sought freedom from the random suffering, they sought to control their environment and so they devised varieties of religious exercises they hoped would appease the gods and protect them.

Then as the tribes began to form alliances and eventually nations, as they developed more control over their environment, they began to develop narratives or myths that made sense of what creation was throwing at them. Those myths also gave them a shared sense of purpose and direction. The nations too came to know their creator, they too sought to understand the work of God in the world, they too sensed an intimacy or union with God.

The narratives that gave them a framework within which to live and love, that gave them purpose and direction, and connected them to the presence of God, finally could not be sustained. In the face of the modernist deconstruction of myth and the postmodern insistence that truth will always remain outside our grasp, the myths became irrelevant; this is as it should be. This is how we evolve, but with that irrelevance came a loss of context and meaning. We see around us right now a culture starved for meaning.

But the good news is that the vast spiritual wasteland is nearing an end. It is unsustainable and so there has been renewed interest in understanding what the ancients were describing, what they were pointing towards when they described God as they did.

There are several themes that emerge over and over

again both cross-culturally and throughout history. The tension between being and becoming is one we have discussed, but there are others. A second major motif is that people describe their experience of God from three perspectives. The three perspectives derive from our language – first person, second person, and third person perspectives on God. We've discovered that each of the great religious traditions point to these three ways of understanding and experiencing the Divine. It seems that each religious tradition emphasizes one of these ways of knowing God over the others, but each found a way to describe the three modes of experience in the only way they could, from within their own worldview. Various theologians and philosophers have worked towards communicating these three understandings of God in a way that makes sense for us today, in our worldview.[36] There has been some generative work done in this area. But before we describe that work, it is best to have a deeper understanding of what has been said in the past.

Much of the Trinitarian conversation over the intervening 1,687 years has been focused on understanding the *being* of God, that is to say, on the static, unchanging, omnipotent, permanent nature of God. The Westminster Confession of Faith, for centuries the standard of reformed theology, spoke of God this way:

> *There is but one only living and true God, who is infinite in being and perfection, a most pure spirit, invisible, without body, parts, or passions, immutable, immense, eternal, incomprehensible, almighty; most wise, most holy, most free, most absolute . . .* [37]

Maybe that's why the Trinity has become so irrelevant in this day and age. The connection between us and this

---
36. Jüurgen Moltmann, Catherine LaCugna, Ken Wilber, Marc Gafni, Alfred North Whitehead, and John Cobb, to name just a few.
37. Westminster Confession of Faith, Chapter II.

God—this "wholly other"—seems tangential at best.

With the understanding of God as permanent *being* outside creation comes a mirror image of the creation. With the traditional "being" understanding of God, creation *is* already actual. The permanent God, outside creation, has created all *things*, including time. As Robert Mesle describes this point of view, "Time has been seen as like a great tapestry woven by God. The tapestry tells a story. But the whole story from beginning to end exists at once on the tapestry. God it is assumed can stand back and see the whole tapestry at once."[38] This is why it was thought the prophets could predict the future. They can simply peer into a future that has already been created by God, as it is revealed to them by God.

Understand that this is a view of creation in which God has already decided who is saved and who is not, who suffers and who does not, which becomes a real problem for modernist sensibilities. For one of the wonderful things that modernism brought into human culture is the ultimate dignity of the individual. It is modernism that gave us our deep concern for human rights, and so the modernist sensibility cannot abide the thought of a God that creates suffering. The idea that God creates suffering is an inevitable conclusion that follows from the assumption that God is a permanent *being* outside creation who created all things, including time.

But suppose, as process theologians do, that *the future does not exist*, but must always be created. We think of a world created out of *things* but if you consider it, there are no "things," if what you mean by a "thing" is something permanent and unchanging. Creation is actually composed of events and processes, of relationships and connections. Mountains are raised by the flow of tectonic plates and worn down by wind and water. Stars live and stars die. There is nothing permanent in all creation. From galaxy clusters to quarks, nothing is permanent. Every "thing" is the product

---

38. C. Robert Mesle, *Process-Relational Philosophy: An Introduction to Alfred North Whitehead*, (West Conshahocken: Templeton Press, 2008), 5.

of a process, a relationship, a connection. It goes all the way down to the fundamentals of reality. The future has not been created because the future is creation's process.

Certainly ideas of *being* have their place. The focus on *becoming* over *being* if pushed too far is, as Ken Wilber puts it, "true but partial." Nevertheless, at the fundamental levels of reality we are becoming. The universe doesn't exist as a permanent thing, it is always becoming.

Our understanding of the nature of God is integral to our understanding of creation. As we shift our thinking about the nature of creation, a very different image of God begins to emerge. God is now fundamentally understood or known in processes and events, relationships and connections. Rather than a God who is "wholly other," disconnected from humanity, unfeeling and judging, this God is intimately connected to us in the darkest moments and in the light. Understand we are no longer talking about the God who is out there. As my friend Marc Gafni says, "the God you don't believe in doesn't exist." We know this God and recognize this God only as we relate, and we do that in three ways.

We know this God in the first person of the Trinity, in the unity of all things, what Whitehead called "the seamless coat of the universe," a unity so profound and so deep as to defy description. This is the non-dual awareness that mystics speak about. It is our true self—the total number of true selves in the world is one! This is the I Am that met Moses in the burning bush. *"God said to Moses, I am who I am. He said further, Thus you shall say to the Israelites, I am has sent me to you."*[39] (To be clear, it's a story; I'm claiming that the story is pointing to the author's experience of the one true self.)

Jesus invites his disciples to participate in the "I Am," in the Gospel of John. *"I will not leave you orphaned; I am coming to you. In a little while the world will no longer see me, but you will see me; because I live, you also will live. On that day you will know that I Am in my Father, and you*

---

39. Exodus 3:14.

in me, and I in you." [40]

Jesus is calling us into a "first-person" relationship to the Divine, or more accurately Jesus is saying that a "first-person" relationship with God is that which defines or creates us. You are at this fundamental, connected level, God.

I know the church has not talked about it that way much and there is a reason for that – our egos. So let me be quick to say that your separate self, that which is disconnected from the presence of God, is not God. But your true self, (and the number of true selves in the universe is precisely one), is God in the first person.

So, there is one God who is known in three persons, each "person" is all of God. As we know God in the first person, the I Am, we are experiencing the entirety of God. I believe that is true; it is also partial.

Trinitarian thinking invites us to seek out two other connections or relationships to the Divine. Process theologians are saying that God receives God's being in becoming and that becoming emerges through events, processes, connections, and relations—relations between an I and a thou. Built into the fabric of creation are relations one to another between unique persons. While it is true that the I Am is the seamless coat of the universe, that coat is not featureless.[41]

The second person of the Trinity, the second person face of God, is incarnate, God interpenetrating creation in a unique form—you, me, the grocer, and the candlestick maker. This face of God is met as each unique-self is created and creating in relationship to the other. This is God expressing God's *agape*, or to put it another way, God is loving each one of us into existence. Understand now that we are not talking about the permanent God residing outside creation; we are talking about the God whose being is known in becoming.

Love is what characterizes the second person relation of the Divine. The literature on the nature of God's love is

---

40. John 14:18-20.
41. Marc Gafni, D.Phil., *Your Unique Self: a Radical Path to Personal Enlightenment* (Tucson, AZ: Integral Publishers, 2012), 7.

extensive. Much has been said about the various Greek words that translate "love," agape and eros being two of those words. I'll not review all that's been said, but there are two aspects of the nature of God's love seen in these words that can help us to live into this second face of the Divine. The Christian scriptures focus on *agape*, but we will see God's love expressed as *eros* in the scriptures as well. *Agape* is the kind of love that sees something and wants to put value into it. This is how I love my children: I seek to give them what they need to flourish.

When we speak of *agape*, we are talking about God giving God's self so as to create a relationship that continually gives life. This is the incarnate, second face of Trinity that Paul speaks about in Philippians.

> *Let the same mind be in you that was in Christ Jesus,*
> *who, though he was in the form of God,*
> *did not regard equality with God*
> *as something to be exploited,*
> *but emptied himself,*
> *taking the form of a slave,*
> *being born in human likeness.*
> *And being found in human form,*
> *he humbled himself . . .* [42]

The Judeo-Christian traditions have emphasized the I-Thou relationship to the Divine sometimes to the exclusion of the other experiences or apprehensions of God. My theology professor once said, "The Doctrine of the Trinity is a lousy definition of God but it does a pretty good job at telling you what you can't say about God."[43] It reminds us not to ask the second person relationship to the Divine to carry all the freight; there is more to knowing God than knowing

---

42. Philippians 2:5-8.
43. Douglas Ottati in a lecture given sometime in 1994.

God as "other." But since it was the second face of God that was emphasized in the Hebrew and Christian myths, when they were deconstructed, so was the ground for an I–Thou relationship to the Divine.

The second person of the Trinity is classically understood as the "Son." But as we recognize the nature of God *becoming* through relationships and connections, it seems more and more that the stories of Jesus showing us the nature of a God who calls us into an I–Thou relationship, a relationship where each of us loved into existence by God, and uniquely becomes the second face of the Divine in relationship to other. In this I–Thou connection, the Divine is becoming in relationship to each unique self.

The other side to God's love, *eros*, is the love that sees something and yearns to enjoy it. The life becoming within us yearns for connection and intimacy with the Divine. This is what the psalmist expressed:

> *As a deer longs for flowing streams,*
> *so my soul longs for you, O God.*
> *My soul thirsts for God*
> *for the living God . . .*[44]

Eros reaches towards the profound unity that lies at the heart of a creation always becoming through relationship and process. It is in the nature of all creation to yearn for this intimacy one to the other and to the Divine. It is in the nature of God to yearn for intimacy and connection with creation, with each unique self. *I am my beloved's, and his desire is for me,*[45] says the poet in the Song of Songs. She has known God's longing for us. Often the message of Christianity has been distorted to mean that God sits in judgment ready to destroy you when in fact God can do nothing but love you, for that is in the nature of God.

The Christian God has often been misrepresented as a

---
44. Psalm 42:1-2.
45. Song of Songs 7:10.

kind of Santa Claus always watching, making that list and checking it twice, ready to do you in when you stray. Instead this God lives to know you. Creation is not a thing that God made. It is not like God made the creation and likes some parts better than other parts. No, creation is made of processes and events, processes and events that are brought into being by the creative love and desire, the very life of God. God's desire for you, the creative breath that animates your life are integral to your becoming. This is not a God who sits outside creation passing judgment on you.

Looked at this way the stories of Jesus are paradigmatic of a new humanity, each of us unique expressions of God's *agape*, each of us with *eros* burning within longing to know God as "other," as "thou." We relate to this God and in so doing we come alive. This is an I-Thou, a second-person relationship with the Divine. It too is complete. The entirety of God is known in an I-Thou relationship.

This idea of relating to the Divine as other is difficult in a world that has deconstructed the myths. So what is meant by relating to God as other? If the God I don't believe in doesn't exist, how can I relate to God?

Let me see if I can give you a glimpse of how one person does it. I once worked with a part-time organist who investigated this question. I called her Saint Kathie; this was not said sarcastically. Kathie was an Elementary School Principal in the District of Columbia—the very definition of a saint. The system seemed to thwart her at every turn. Nevertheless she worked tirelessly for the children and teachers in her charge. She did right by them.

At one point, Kathie wondered about the power of prayer and whether it could change things. She decided to keep track of the prayers she offered and the answers she "received." All she had lying about was a teacher's grading book, so she set it up with one column for the date, one to describe her prayer request, and the third to keep track of the answer—positive or negative. When she told me about the project, I did a double take. "Let me get this straight Kathie, you're giving

God a grade?"

She told me that while it may have started that way, something else happened as she engaged in this practice. She said that as she kept track of the prayers over time, it was as though she could discern the subtle movements of God within our world. As she paid attention to what was happening, she had a greater understanding of the direction God was moving in her life. Instead of watching to see whether God would live up to her expectations, she came to understand God's influence in her life more. As one prayer was answered in a way that surprised her, that gave her information about how God is working in her life. As God seemed silent on another prayer, again she took that as more information that helped her to understand the movements of Spirit in the world. She stopped looking for the cosmic bellhop, that God who does our bidding (some of the time), and instead accepted the reality that God moves without altering the fabric of creation precisely because God moves in the process of creating. Over time Kathie found she was more able to pray in harmony with the dynamic, creative, power of God. The practice, rather than reinforcing a magical view of God, had moved her into an I-Thou engagement with the mystery of God. It changed her and allowed her to live life with a greater sense of God's presence in the whole of life.

Before we move on to the third person of the Trinity something else must be said of the second person, the second face of God, for in it we find the ground of ethics. Each of us is a unique expression of God's love. Each of us is literally being loved into existence. Each of us is created with yearning for connection. The dance of *agape* and *eros* takes place in the formation of the I-Thou relationship that gives us life. When we live outside that dance of love, we lose our life. Literally, to live outside of the harmony of God's creation, outside of the relationships that give us life, is to lose our life.

Each and every one of us has been and is being loved into existence by the love of God such that when we tear the fabric of creation, when we distort or destroy the relationships that make up creation, we are violating the source of life itself. Each person we see is a unique expression of the Divine love dance. Each person is valuable beyond belief. We see in the other, the face of God and so we are called to live in love with all creatures, with all creation. For creation in its entirety is the continual loving of God, who is drawing all things together in perfect harmony. A creative, loving response is demanded from us. It is our obligation. This is the ground of ethics. To know God in the second person is to recognize our relationship to all that is. It calls us to express the love created within us. That's the place of "law" in the Hebrew and Christian scriptures. It is expressing the love that creates us. To live outside of this I-Thou relationship breaks God's law; it is unethical.

The dignity of each unique self matters because each unique self is an expression of the love of God. Without each person living her or his unique expression of God's love, creation itself cannot be complete.

There is one God who is known in three persons, yet each "person" is all of God. As we know God in the second person, the incarnate, interpenetrating presence of God, we know the entirety of God. That's true, but it is also only partial.

We move then to the third person of the Trinity, the Holy Spirit. How are we to know the Spirit?

Every day I look at the Astronomy Picture of the Day from NASA.[46] Each day a picture of the cosmos—galaxies, comets, planets—"star rising after star and constellation after constellation as the immensity of this bewildering universe looms up before our staggered mind."[47] This is the third face of God—an I–It relationship to the Divine.

People tell me that they know God when they are in nature. To be sure this is true; they are knowing the third face

---

46. http://apod.nasa.gov/apod/
47. Arthur J. Gossip, "But When Life Tumbles in, What Then?" in *A Treasury of Great Preaching, Volume VIII* (Dallas: Word Publishing, 1995), 232.

of the Divine. We see it in the way biological systems evolve. We see it in the creative inventiveness of humans. This is the Divine that shimmers in the midst of all reality, the Divine love that drives evolution forward. This is the face of God that carries the "whole creation [that] has been groaning in labor pains,"[48] into a new tomorrow.

The entire creation is evolving. The relationships, processes, events, and connections are ever becoming and unfolding into the future, and it is the Spirit of God, the third face of God, that moves all of those connections into the future. Andrew Cohen describes it this way: "But if one is able to stay perfectly in that Emptiness, there is a quality that begins to manifest right above the surface. It has something to do with the source of all life, with Love, and with an evolutionary impulse."[49]

There is one God who is known in three persons, yet each "person" is all of God. As we know God in the third person, the evolutionary impulse, we know the entirety of God. While I believe that is true, it is also partial.

Traditionally the Doctrine of the Trinity has focused on the being of God. But through the centuries reflections on it have also focused on hierarchy. Father, then Son, then Holy Spirit, in that order. It raises interesting questions about the nature of reality. In our postmodern world we rail at the notion of hierarchy and for good reason. An "orthodox" view of the Trinity must call hierarchy into question and in fact a good amount of work has been done to reclaim the doctrine from its patriarchal past. Catherine LaCugna in particular has helped us to see that the three persons of the Trinity are in an ever-flowing dance, a "perichoresis"[50] of perspectives on the Divine.[51]

---

48. Romans 8:22.
49. Carter Phipps, *Evolutionaries* (New York: Harper Perennial, 2012), 318.
50. See Catherine LaCugna's seminal work, *God With Us, the Trinity and Christian Life* (San Francisco: HarperCollins, 1973).
51. It is certainly true that three co-equal, "co-complete" visions the Divine cannot give free reign to the notions of hierarchy. So we are remiss in look-

It is my understanding that all the world's great religious traditions have a place for all three perspectives. It also seems to be the case that each tends to "major" in one or another. The classical eastern traditions tend to major in a first person perspective of God. The Judeo-Christian tradition tends to major in a second person relationship to God. The "native" traditions and the modern academy tend to major in a third person relationship to God—whether they express it that way or not.

But here is the point: while it has not worked out in practice, the doctrine of the Trinity encourages us to take all three perspectives seriously. It suggests that we can enter the whole of God through any of the perspectives but that we are impoverished to remain sequestered there. For it is in the dance that we come to know and live our purpose of becoming beloved, I Am, the next beautiful expression of the love of God.

---

ing at the world as a series of hierarchical relationships, but it is also true that the three faces of the Divine have particular roles and those roles are at times in hierarchical relationship. In that our view of the creative order mirrors our view of the Divine we might do well to consider how hierarchy does play out in a healthy becoming.

CHAPTER 9

The Trouble with Sin

The foundational text for this chapter is the fall of Adam and Eve. The event this story described never happened. It's a story that tries to tell us something about the human condition, but it's still just a story.

> *They heard the sound of the Lord God walking in the garden at the time of the evening breeze, and the man and his wife hid themselves from the presence of the Lord God among the trees of the garden. But the Lord God called to the man, and said to him, "Where are you?" He said, "I heard the sound of you in the garden, and I was afraid, because I was naked; and I hid myself." He said, "Who told you that you were naked? Have you eaten from the tree of which I commanded you not to eat?" The man said, "The woman whom you gave to be with me, she gave me fruit from the tree, and I ate." Then the Lord God said to the woman, "What is this that you have done?" The woman said, "The serpent tricked me, and I ate."*
>
> *The Lord God said to the serpent, "Because you have done this, cursed are you among all animals and among all wild creatures; upon your belly you shall go, and dust you shall eat*

all the days of your life.
I will put enmity between you and the woman,
and between your offspring and hers;
he will strike your head,
and you will strike his heel."
To the woman he said,
"I will greatly increase your pangs in childbearing;
in pain you shall bring forth children,
yet your desire shall be for your husband,
and he shall rule over you."
And to the man he said,
"Because you have listened to the voice of your wife,
and have eaten of the tree
about which I commanded you,
'You shall not eat of it,'
cursed is the ground because of you;
in toil you shall eat of it all the days of your life;
thorns and thistles it shall bring forth for you;
and you shall eat the plants of the field.
By the sweat of your face
you shall eat bread
until you return to the ground,
for out of it you were taken;
you are dust,
and to dust you shall return."

Genesis 3:8-19

Liberal Christians, well, really all Christians, like to emphasize the idea that God is love. But it gets complicated, because love, and law, and judgment, and sin are all somehow related throughout the scriptures. This passage about Adam and Eve for instance: it's a far cry from "God is love,"[52] a far cry. God is love. God is agape. If eros is one kind of love,

---

52. Found in I John 4:16. The Greek word used for "love" is agape, which is interesting because the Christian Scriptures never use the word "eros" to describe love. That's a subject for another day.

The Trouble with Sin

agape is another kind of love. Eros is: I see an object and I want to enjoy the value in it. My brother-in-law made a great roasted turkey last week. I love turkey and I enjoyed it. On the other hand agape is that love where I see an object and I want to put value into it. For some people that's a blank canvas; for some people that's a child that they want to raise up to become everything that he or she might be. See an object and put value into it and that's the God that is love.[53]

That love of God is all around us. But is the Bible talking out of two sides of its mouth? On the one hand, you've got God is Love always putting value into us and on the other hand you seem to have a God who is making his list and checking it twice.

You get the lump of coal and judgment of some kind. This is one way to interpret the Bible when you read those passages about judgment. The people have sinned and therefore God judges them. The trouble is, this word 'sin' has taken on a wrong meaning in our culture. Therefore, we feel that God is a judging God we feel guilty about the sin, (or of course some blow the whole thing off, don't feel guilty, and act without any ground for ethics). But some of us feel ashamed, deeply ashamed about the sin or the flaws within us and feel that we can't possibly be loved by God. Some of us feel quite self-righteous because we don't sin as much as the next person. Some of us are angry about the way it all works out, thinking 'Well God knows what's going on, God understands, God has his reasons for taking life or giving life.' "Sin"— an unfortunate word I'd say, but we use it a lot in the Christian church. So I thought we'd do well to look at it a bit. What is it, this sin, this sin that causes righteous anger and guilt and depression and everything else?

When I was a kid I thought sin is the bad things people do. I learned that from my friend, Jimmy. Jimmy was a Roman Catholic. Every Thursday afternoon Jimmy would go to

---

53. I think "love" is more complex than all that. Clearly there is a dance between eros and agape that we know in the character of God, but that too is a subject for another day.

confession. We used to wonder why he would do that. "Isn't the priest going to tell your mother," I asked Jimmy, "What do you confess anyway?" Jimmy said, "Well this week I cussed once and I hit my little brother pretty hard, and I came home late for dinner with mud on me, I'll confess that." So I got it. Sin is the bad things people do.

He went and confessed. But here's the thing: I was there the night that Jimmy came home for dinner late with mud on him.

It was like this: we had another friend, Frankie. Frankie, Jimmy and I decided to go out pollywog hunting. We got a couple of coffee cans and went out to Housel's Pond. Housel's Pond is fed by a stream . . . actually more like a small river of thick and sticky black muck. We put a little plank over it so you could kneel down with your coffee can, dip it in and see if you could find some pollywogs. Now I want you to picture this. We were about nine years old and my buddy Frankie was kneeling down on a plank. His coffee can was stuck deep into the muck and his butt was stuck way up in the air. . . Well I don't know what got into me exactly, but somehow Frankie ended up falling into all that black muck.

It turned out that wasn't so clever of me because Frankie was about a year older than me and about twice my size. Once he got himself out of all that muck, he chased me down and dragged me back kicking and screaming, laughing and hollering, and pulled me into the muck. He dunked me all the way under. I was a complete mess. So there we were standing in the river of muck and we looked up on the bank and there is Jimmy, still very clean. He was also laughing at us. Can you imagine what happened next?

It's true that Jimmy went home for dinner late that night with black muck all over him. But I ask you, exactly whose sin was he confessing the following Thursday? It's just more complicated than that. It is not about whether you did something or I did something because there is always some sort of corporate responsibility.[54]

There is always that sense of corporate responsibility. That's certainly how the Bible looks at it. The story we read about Adam and Eve is part of the series of stories about the Fall in Genesis 3 to 11. It's really a several-step fall. We start with Adam and Eve. There is this alienation between them and God. God used to come down and hang out in the Garden with them. We have a picture of a lovely sort of intimacy. Then it gets fractured. The relationship is torn apart. That's the sadness. Human beings are not in intimate communion with God. (Not that we ever were; the story is really about the enduring human condition, not what happened once upon a time.)

Adam and Eve have a couple of kids, and what happens? One murders the other. The result of the initial alienation continued. Then we read another story in the Bible . . . about the Nephilim. These huge god-like creatures, and the Bible says they were with the daughters of men. (Nobody knows what that means, but whatever it is, rest assured it's not good.) Then there is Noah. Things have gotten so bad that God says, "Can I find one or two righteous people and start over? This whole Adam and Eve thing hasn't worked out too well." So the floods come. They come from the heavens.

I think I've mentioned that the way people back then understood how the universe is built is you have this flat land. Then you have this dome over the land. God had separated the waters below the land from the waters above the land. Up above was water and above that was where God was. God opened the windows of heaven, it says in the Bible, and all the water come pouring back in.

So God starts over with Noah, but it turns out that relationship didn't work that well either. The next thing you know humans are developing a society that decides to build a tower to the heavens. Why was this a bad idea? Because

---

54. For the moment we can leave unanswered the question of whether or not a nine year-old boy getting muddy can really be classified as a sin. (I guess Jimmy's mom thought so. I don't.)

they wanted to break through the dome and take over God's domain. Human beings, when left to their own devices, when alienated from God, ended up doing battle with, rather than being in communion with, the Divine. We're always fighting against the creative purposes of God.

That's the problem. It starts with an alienation from God and it moves from one person to another person until finally it covers the whole world. Frankie is in the mud (my fault); he pulls me in; and together we pull Jimmy in. That's the problem of sin, and it has consequences.

The ancients understood this. They understood that there were consequences for actions. They also struggled with the fact that some of the suffering in life seemed dis-attached from the consequences of our behavior. But their concept of God moved them to put the onus of all that on God. They made it all God's responsibility. They were trying to figure out how much of what happens to us is the result of consequences of actions, meaning we were bad and so God sent some sort of judgment on us, and how much of it is because God is God and does stuff?

That's what the whole book of Job is about. It is trying to understand how a righteous person can be judged. The Hebrews had this tension in their understanding between the sense that there are consequences for their actions, but there are also things that happen that are not directly related to who we are or what we do.

We look at God a bit differently than they did. We don't see a dome up there with windows in it. We have a much larger perspective on what creation is and what the divine creative force is all about. I do not think of a God that controls every little thing so that all the suffering that happens is deserved. God did not "take this or that person, at this or that time." Rather there is death and life and that is all part of the whole creative process. Things happen. Accidents happen. It is not something God has perpetrated on us because we did something wrong—because we sinned.

But even when the Hebrews blamed God for everything,

they still were able to discern God's loving purpose. They know that at center, God's grace comes first. This thoroughgoing understanding is built into the very fabric of the Bible from start to finish. Let me explain by going back to those stories in Genesis.

At the end of the Adam and Eve story, we learn that after the judgment the snake will crawl on its belly, the woman will have pain in child birth, and the man is going to have to work really hard in order to get food. But . . . after God passed that judgment God is very concerned. God was concerned that the man and woman would re-enter the garden and eat from the tree of life so that they would live forever. We often read the story as God laying out one more punishment, but that's not what the story is getting at. God did not want the man and woman to have to live in their distorted state indefinitely so God stops that from happening by putting a guard up at the entrance to the garden. It is in fact good news that God keeps Adam and Eve from coming back into the garden and living forever in their distorted state.

Next story: When Cain slew Abel, he said, "The punishment is more than I can bear. My life is forfeit." But God didn't want that to happen and so put a mark on Cain to protect him. There's a little piece of grace at the end of that story as though to assure Cain, "God is going to continue to stay with you no matter what."

We get to Noah, and what do we have at the end of that story? Most people know this—a rainbow. God has, metaphorically speaking, taken "His" bow and arrow and put it up in the sky saying, "I'm not going to annihilate humanity again. If this act of judgment doesn't work I'll do something different."

Then there's the tower of Babel. In that story the people try to take over God's domain? Disastrous. People in charge of creation? So what does God do? God confuses their language and they scatter all over the place.

Richard Escher has a wonderful engraving that tells that story. The tower is so perfectly built, everything is so even and nice—until you get into the upper stages of it. Then the bricks start getting crooked and finally it's just not done. There are tools scattered all over and everybody is gone. The thing about that story that's so sad is that there is no grace at the end. They're done. Humankind is scattered across the whole earth. . . .

That is until you get to Genesis, Chapter 12, verse 1. Then God calls to Abram and tells him to go into the promised land so that I can make a people of you, people that are united with me, that are not alienated from the Divine. The entire rest of the Bible is about God trying to create a people that will not be alienated from the Divine. To be clear, that story is not written so you and I will know what happened to those early Israelites. First of all, scholars tell us that most of it didn't happen; it's a story. But the story is our story. It is written so we'll know how God works in our lives. It's all about God's creative purpose. Even judgment passages are like that—stories that tell us that God's grace comes first. God continually moves into our lives. God seeks only to restore us and bring us back, so that when we are restored, when we are united with the Divine, we will be made complete and whole. God's purposes will not be thwarted. I know that interpretation doesn't seem to sit on the surface of the text but that's because the stories were written a very long time ago with a very different set of cultural, economic, political, and natural assumptions in place. Nevertheless God's primary grace is thoroughgoing from Genesis to Revelation.

Some people suggest that a God so focused on law and law breaking cannot be a gracious God but nothing could be farther from the truth. The Jewish people, the same people that offered us this understanding of God's deep desire to be united with us, also gave us the law. It is summarized as "Love God and love neighbor." The law is essentially about allowing the creative power of God to move into us and fill us up so that it can overflow our hearts and we can share it with the people around us. Law is good news because the nature of God is love.

At the end of that long-ago afternoon at Housel's Pond,

The Trouble with Sin

Frankie, and Jimmy and I were covered in muck. We were walking home and felt a little uncomfortable. It had been a long hot day, my bones were aching, and we were getting just a little concerned about what our parents might say when they saw us covered in mud . . . and worse, we were late. As we were walking along I remember we didn't say a whole lot. We were just a tad depressed. We rounded the bend on Grenville Road and there we saw Frankie's dad – to this day I call him Papa T. He was walking back and forth behind that old Toro mower, cutting the grass. He took one look at us and started to laugh. "Gentlemen, hold it right there. I'm gettin' the camera." Grace abounds.

This is the picture he took that day; I'm the boy on the right.

So Papa T took our picture and brought us around back. He got out the garden hose, and started washing us off. All the aches in my body started to loosen up and we laughed and splashed around and had a fabulous time. (I remember though that Papa T didn't think it was a good idea to jump into the above-ground pool just then.)

That's the nature of God—to take you from whatever state you are in and take you around back and start to wash you off and help you heal and feel better.

The reason I'm telling you that is because most of us are hurt at a pretty deep level. All of us. There are wounds that we carry, fears that we carry, things we're ashamed of that we're not going to let anybody know. There are things that make us shiver in the night, things that sometimes make us drink too much because we need to soothe the pain that comes up, and things that make us really angry so we lash out. That's how sin goes from one person to another to another.

The reason I'm telling you this is because it is in God's nature to want to look at you where you are. Whether you come in second or whether you feel as if you're seriously flawed, this is a God who will always bring you around back, who will always bring out the hose, and will always start the process of cleaning you off. The Bible doesn't talk out of two sides of its mouth. The entire story is about God's love. That's why I like it so much.

CHAPTER 10

Does Prayer Work?

"I have given them your word, and the world has hated them because they do not belong to the world, just as I do not belong to the world. I am not asking you to take them out of the world, but I ask you to protect them from the evil one. They do not belong to the world, just as I do not belong to the world. Sanctify them in the truth; your word is truth. As you have sent me into the world, so I have sent them into the world. And for their sakes I sanctify myself, so that they also may be sanctified in truth.

"I ask not only on behalf of these, but also on behalf of those who will believe in me through their word, that they may all be one. As you, Abba, are in me and I am in you, may they also be in us, so that the world may believe that you have sent me. The glory that you have given me I have given them, so that they may be one, as we are one, I in them and you in me, that they may become completely one, so that the world may know that you have sent me and have loved them even as you have loved me. Abba, I desire that those also, whom you have given me, may be with me where I am, to see my glory, which you have given me because you loved me before the foundation of the world.

"Righteous Abba, the world does not know you, but I know you; and these know that you have sent me.

> *I made your name known to them, and I will make it known, so that the love with which you have loved me may be in them, and I in them."*
>
> John 17:14-26

It used to be that we had a God up there that we could depend upon to do things for us. You want to get healed, you pray to this God, this God reaches in and fixes things up and heals you. Or, you want to keep the bad weather away; you pray hard enough, the bad weather will not come your way.

This is the God my father refers to as the cosmic bellhop. (I think he got that from J. B. Phillips.) Let's face it: there is no God up there, above a dome, that fidgets and fiddles with things. I think there is enough scientific observation around to do away with that picture of God. But what do we put in its place?

Perhaps God is a kind of power, or creative force, a movement of Grace that allows for creation to grow and emerge and become something wonderful and new. Some would say creation emerges from the being of God, that the Divine is like a river of Grace, a force, an "other," who is drawing the chain of cause and effect towards God's own purpose.

However we describe this God, this creative drive of the Universe, the method of creation is a little messy. It emerges out of chaos and it takes a long time. In fact, the most recent estimate is that creation has taken 13.82 billion years to get to this moment. Whatever "God" is like, then, God is not deterministic, not in "full control," so we can't really blame everything on this God, neither can we give this God all the credit.

The moment I start conceptualizing a God that is not omnipotent, not "in charge" in that magical way we've imagined, I've done away with a lifetime of habits. It is hard to replace that omnipotent God "up there" in our imaginations! That is especially true since the old traditional language provides us with such good metaphors for engaging God. For instance, a Father in heaven is powerful and personal, a wonderful metaphor, assuming it is not used exclusively and that it doesn't represent something hurtful and oppressive for you.[55] Jesus can be those footprints in the sand, that ever-present Lord and guide. After all, it worked for us for thousands of years.

Yet, here we are. It creates a profound challenge for us, a challenge that comes into focus when I ask, "Why do we pray? If there is no God waiting in the wings to alter the course of history when we pray, then why do we pray?"

I wish I could offer you an answer. I can't—at least not a satisfying answer, because the answer that we "need" would in the end provide a technological explanation of how prayer works. There are plenty of researchers working on this explanation. There is all kinds of research about prayer and healing,[56] about particular kinds of prayer, whether or not some kinds of prayer work better than others, whether trained spiritual masters' prayer is more effective than yours or mine. Over time I think we'll figure out a technology for praying. We will one day know how our minds, as they express intention, have an impact on the world around us. But right now we don't have one, so it is very difficult for me to tell you why we pray. All I can do is share with you why I pray and that is an evolving story. It has changed even while I've gone through the process of writing this text.

I pray because water is wet. I pray because when I see novelty, like the first surprising wetness, that's when I see the power of God at work. I pray because I want to connect to that which is pulling creation forward. Novelty! What on earth would make us think that a bunch of chemicals, lying around in a pool of water, would become something else,

---

55. Many relate quite deeply to this "Father." I find that in my darkest moments it gives me solace and strength. Even though I almost never use it in public worship, or much in private for that matter, I'd be loath to do without it.

56. Pick up anything by Dr. Larry Dossey. He does a good job of gathering current evidence and organizing it into a coherent narrative.

let alone replicate themselves and produce enough oxygen to block out some of the UV rays coming in from the sun? That's what happened and allowed still more slime mold to grow, and each of these little organisms developed a separate identity. Identity! Where did that come from? It's an emergent property like wetness.

Of course the emergent property of identity has created its own share of problems. That's the thing with an evolving creation. That slime mold that grew so well produced enough oxygen to pollute the atmosphere; the mold began to suffocate themselves. Sound familiar? It created a problem that evolution had to fix with the advent of animal cells that use oxygen. But if I have an identity, I want to protect mine even if that means getting rid of yours. That's a problem evolution needs to contend with.

Still it's really quite remarkable. This separate identity property has produced birds that can fly, fish that can see with electricity, bats that can see with sonar. It has produced vertebrates, invertebrates, and eventually it produced us, homo sapiens. Along the way a whole new property emerged – self-consciousness. Is there anything that would suggest to you that just because our brains are configured in this particular way, we would be conscious, aware of ourselves existing in a fabric of time and space? Consciousness is an emergent property. I couldn't have predicted it. Yet, there it is, consciousness brought to you by the power that drives creation forward.

Now here is the real trick. Because we have consciousness, because we have minds, not just brains, we can produce novelty of a sort, all by ourselves. We can produce it. We have ideas and can make them happen.

I heard this great story on NPR the other day, radiolab.org. There were bio-engineering students at MIT who were growing e-coli bacteria in a petri dish so that they could use them for experiments. They had the e-coli in the petri dish. Apparently they also had a bit too much time on their hands as they waited for them to grow because they kept thinking of novel things they could do – things that had not been done.[57]

I don't know if you know this, but e-coli bacteria really stink. They smell revolting and naturally that made the lab pretty unpleasant, so the students got to thinking. They ended up writing to someone at the University of Kansas who was working on the genes of Petunias. The MIT students got them to send a little piece of DNA from the Petunia then took that DNA and put it in the e-coli bacteria. As the culture grew, the one with this new DNA, it started to smell like wintergreen. Surprising. Novelty.

The e-coli still had finished growing and they still had too much time on their hands, so they came up with another idea. "Maybe we don't need to keep watching and waiting for the culture to grow. Maybe we could develop some sort of signal that the bacteria has finished growing so we can go outside and relax," (or whatever MIT students do). So they got another piece of genetic material, stuck it in the e-coli bacteria that already smelled like wintergreen. As long as the culture was growing it smelled like wintergreen, but when it stopped growing it smelled like bananas. Again, novelty.

The same processes, that is processes characterized by novel moves forward, forms us. You and I are formed in part by the genetic material with which we were born, in part by the world around us, and in part by the emergent ideas of our culture. It's amazing really. We are not predetermined from the start. Events and influences can still impact our development and evolution, because eventually external events and circumstances will feed back and impact our biology. That's the way things are set up. What that means is that you and I are "created co-creators." That's the way Phillip Heffner puts it.[58] We have emerged as created co-creators. We are now participating in creating who we are and this at a time when we must evolve beyond our biologically determined behaviors or risk the collapse of the whole planet.

---

57. http://www.radiolab.org/story/91596-so-called-life/
58. Philip Heffner, *The Human Factor, Theology and the Sciences* (Minneapolis: Augsburg Press, 2000).

What is next? What's the next emergent property? What will move us beyond survival of the fittest, a law that is leading us toward Armageddon? Are we forever going to live with the fallout from competition? Are we always and forever going to strive to become bigger and better than the other guy? Is there always going to be economic strife—always the poor and the rich? And are we ever going to get past arguing about my religion being better than your religion, as though Christianity could make it to the top of the heap, surviving because it is the fittest religion? Is that what is going to happen? Or might something new emerge, might something brand new emerge out of this conscious group of people?

This is the very thing that Jesus is addressing in the gospel text with which I started this chapter. Jesus has a vision for a new emerging property. Oh, I know he wouldn't have called it that, but that's what it is. It is something brand new and hopeful. He was living in a world where survival of the fittest was the way it was and it wasn't pretty. He saw military power oppressing people. He saw a split between the classes, and he saw people claiming, with the power of the cross behind them, that one religion was better than another. He saw people being driven apart and not drawn together.

Jesus saw a different creative possibility. He looked at creation from a profound connection to the creator and he could see God's hand in the creative possibilities of the moment, he could hear the voice speaking creative words that set new evolutionary moments in motion. That's what Jesus heard. Jesus knew the voice of love, the voice of novelty and hope and life. He recognized the emergent properties, the creative possibilities of a human being open to the love of God. He knew that a group of people formed in that love, powered by the creative Word would hear the call and live out their unique purpose. As created co-creators they would reach into creative possibility, live in the beauty and the wonder and the goodness of all creation.

This is glory that Jesus knew: the opportunity to be filled so full of the love of God that it overflows into the world around us and in its wake will come infinite creative possibility.

"They do not belong to the world," he said (John 17:15). They are not of the world where survival of the fittest is the order of the day. They are of a different world, formed in a different way. They are formed by the Logos, by the Truth, by the power inherent to God's love. Jesus knows that when the disciples' lives are clear of what binds them, they will see the glory of God. It is this we are becoming and Jesus prays in order to join in the project. He is calling forth the Spirit within him and within each of us.

So, why do I pray? I pray because at this moment in the creative story of life on our planet I'm called upon to co-create with that which creates. Praying means getting into sync with the Holy, creative presence of the Divine. Praying itself sets us in the stream of the One whose love we express and so it contributes to the new, emergent life that Jesus envisioned. That's why I pray.

But another deeper reason to pray has emerged within me these last months. I pray because it works. The question is what do I mean by "it works" if I don't think God is going to alter the course of history in order to answer my prayer? The reality is that that question can only be answered from within the life of faith, because the answer comes only when you clear the "eye of the Spirit." What I mean is this: when we engage God, we come to know God and more and more we take an active role in the creative process. Don't roll your eyes quite yet, I know the weakness of the argument. I know that the modern mind will then say, "Well of course, you project your hopes onto the cosmos and lo and behold they are reflected back." From that point of view, you are absolutely right.

But just because I'm projecting that hope does not mean what is returned is not real. There is no verifiable evidence that can distinguish between my projection, a deep desire to know God and live in communication with God, and the reality of what then lives and grows within me. There is no way to "know" the difference, at least if what you mean by "know" is establish it by verifiable experimentation. That is certainly one kind of knowing and it is the only kind that some will rely on. But there are many ways to "know" something. I know my wife loves me, but I don't know that because I've measured her hormone levels, or read her mind. I know because my heart knows.

It is that way with God, and the interesting thing is that humanity has been affirming that truth for thousands of years. Human beings from all over the globe have been praying for thousands of years, and for thousands of years they have found what they have believed to be a real knowing of God. Perhaps we can write off the mythic tales they tell, but to deny the depth of their experience without a second thought would, I think, be tantamount to sticking our heads in the sand.

Why pray? The answer comes when we live in relationship to God, when we spend time with God. People do that in a variety of ways. Earlier I spoke about the Trinity and how it opens up three approaches to the presence of God. I've come to believe that each of us has a preferred way of entering into relation with the Divine. When I study and even imbibe creation with my heart open and my mind available to wonder, I sense the presence of God. It almost shimmers throughout reality. I study history in the same way and I can sense the presence of the Divine right there. It is at that moment that my relationship with God begins to expand. I take the first steps into redeveloping a second person relationship with God. I can pray to the one that lives and breathes in the midst of everything. As that communication develops, I begin to speak my intentions to the Divine, and my faith grows, my faith in a creation that is unfolding before us. Then the creative possibilities seem limitless.

From within that relationship, prayer connects me to the purpose and direction of God. Remember, we are each a unique expression of the Divine, and so as we pray, we are expressing the desires of God. This brings us back to the question of, how does prayer work? I said at the beginning that I expect there is a technology, a mechanism that prayer operates in a particular way. I expect we'll come to understand how that mechanism works one day, but when we do it will only be half the story. When we do we will know how it works, but we will never know God's creative ways within it, those we are able to see only with the eye of Spirit, those we will see only as we move into relationship with all that is. That clarity comes when we pray as an undeniably unique expression of the One from whom all things come. That's why I am learning to pray once again.

PART III

SO WHAT DOES THIS DEMAND OF US?

The world is in outrageous pain and the necessary response is outrageous love. Each of us is a unique expression of the creative love of the God that Christians have come to know in Jesus the Christ. Each of us has unique gifts and unique opportunities to act in the world so that the outrageous pain may be healed.

But it is more than that. It is not just that we are a unique expression of the love intelligence of the universe and that we have an opportunity to heal the pain, but that we have a unique obligation to do so. This isn't optional. The world cannot be complete, the world cannot come to fruition in its glorious hope and beauty without you, without you performing your unique obligation.

So let me ask you this: what outrages you? When you look at the outrageous pain that permeates human society, when you look at the outrageous pain inflicted upon the cosmos, what is it that outrages you? If you can answer that, you may well have found that place in the world that needs your incredibly gorgeous gift of love.

I am outraged that Christianity, a beautiful religious

framework that could support the development and growth of billions of people, that could bring the power of God into the lives of so many, is instead a laughing stock in most of modern culture. To be clear, I do not blame that on modern culture. The church has blown it by refusing to take seriously the modern critique and develop new intelligible language that points the way for a modern society. The church has lost track of the fact that it does not exist for itself. It exists to bring good news into the world, the news that we are each an expression of God's creative love and have the power to create what is beautiful and whole. Part III suggests we should get to it.

CHAPTER 11

Wake Up, Grow Up, Show Up[59]

> *But to all who received the logos* [this pattern or driving force in creation], *to all who received him, who trusted in his name, he gave power to become children of God.*
>
> John 1:12

I have described the cross and resurrection, the central motif of Christian religion, as being descriptive of the process of evolution. Cross and resurrection are the movement from death to life, but more than that they're a movement from death to a *new* life, to something novel, something unexpected, something our imaginations can neither create nor predict. That newness seems to come out of nowhere, like when you put two hydrogen atoms and an oxygen atom together and you get water. If we had been there to watch the first water molecules come into being, and we were very, very, clever, we might have predicted that those two hydrogen atoms would stick to that oxygen atom to make a molecule, but without having seen it before, we would not have predicted the property of flow. That is *new* creation.

Who would have predicted that the single-celled organisms that once upon a time floated about in the midst of the

---

59. Wake Up, Grow Up, Show Up is almost a shorthand description of what's come to be called the Unique Self dharma as formulated by Dr. Marc Gafni. In that this book is effectively a Christian exposition of that dharma, this serves as a kind of summary of where we've come thus far.

oceans would come together and form cooperative entities? Probably not without having seen "cooperation" before. We would not have predicted cooperation and we certainly would not have imagined that those cooperatives might become entities in their own right, with each cell playing a specialized role. That's amazing enough when you ponder it, but creation was far from being done. Something enormously novel occurred. It is not simply that cells formed cooperatives and specialization so that plants and animals evolved. This next thing was of a different type. The brain developed with its trillions of synapses firing, more than the grains of sands on the earth, we're told, and out of that brain emerged a self-consciousness being—a being who can grasp time, a being who can feel separation, a being who can perceive something beyond itself. Why is that a different type of creation entirely? Because now the universe has created something that can see and love the universe; this creation can relate to its Creator. But it's not just that. The astounding, and perhaps terrifying, thing is that we are now cognizant of our own evolution and so we can participate in the creative evolutionary process. As the Apostle Paul put it, "So if anyone is in Christ, there is a new creation: everything old has passed away; see, everything has become new."[60] All of this takes place through the process of evolution. One thing dies and gives way for the next to emerge, each step transcending and including the step before, each step self-organizing into increasingly complex entities, each step a novel and unpredictable moment in creation.

The creative moments of cross and resurrection have these three characteristics as well. It's a moment where life transcends yet includes what went before. It's a moment of increasing complexity or self-organization. And it's a novel moment in creation, one we couldn't have predicted from the evidence at hand. This is a very different way of looking at Christian theology, to be sure, and I am not suggesting that the people who developed the Christian doctrines of salvation

---

60. 2 Corinthians 5:17.

or sanctification were aware they were living in an evolving universe. It seems clear to me they did not think so. They didn't have the knowledge or the language or the ideas to think that way. They did, however, have a very real experience of living in communion with God and so they described those experiences or intuitions in the best way, in fact in the only way, they knew how and that was from within their own thought world.

They could not describe a world in which the God drew creation towards God's own end through a chain of cause and effect that involved a molecule shaped in a double helix folded over itself. You can't talk about DNA if you think the world is made up of four elements—earth, fire, air and water—or that blood has magical properties. You can't talk about the rise of testosterone in men in places of authority as impacting their behavior[61] while at the same time speaking of a world entirely controlled by spiritual entities. You talk about God in terms that are familiar to you. You can talk about a very real experience of the Divine in ways that make sense to you. That is what the early theologians did. That is what we must do.

The words we use to describe God and God's interaction with creation will surely be different than those the biblical authors used, but to be Christian is to point towards the same gracious, loving, creative God they knew and we know. This is the nature of theological conversation. To that end, I will put these descriptions of God's love and grace in light of our understanding of evolution side by side with traditional understandings of Christian faith.

First, we're going to talk about how an evolutionary understanding of Christianity will sit side by side with the doctrine of salvation, that is, the doctrine that describes how we are saved and what we are saved from. Next we will reflect on the doctrine of sanctification, that is, the doctrine concerning how we are transformed or perfected by the power

---

61. As discussed in Michael Dowd, *Thank God for Evolution: How the Marriage of Science and Religion Will Transform Your Life and Our World* (New York, New York: Viking, The Penguin Group, 2007), 161.

of God. Then finally we'll reflect on eschatology, that is, the words we use to talk about the end times— Jesus' second coming, so to speak.

First the doctrine of salvation. We are saved, the tradition tells us, from something called sin. Actually the Apostle Paul refers to it as *hamartia*, which many people have pointed out is an archery term for "missing the mark." Sin is often thought of as the bad things people do, but traditional Christian theology would suggest it is something much deeper than that. We might call it "the human problem." The Unique Self teaching would see it, at least in part, as a reflection of the false self. There are many ways to describe it, but I think the Apostle Paul gets it at pretty well. He describes sin almost as an infection that so alters us that we cannot do the good we want to do. That's how he puts it in the seventh chapter of Romans. *"For I do not do the good I want, but the evil I do not want is what I do. Now if I do what I do not want, it is no longer I that do it, but sin that dwells within me"* (Romans 7:19).

So sin runs deep. That presents a problem for the traditional Christian who also believes God's justice demands retribution for the things we do as a result of that infection. When we break God's law, something the infected human inevitably does, then blood must be shed to balance the scales of justice. Bear with me here: all I'm trying to do is describe a traditional formulation of the doctrine of salvation.

The scriptures tell the story of this infection, its consequences, and God's response to it. They suggest that there was a point in time when human beings were not infected by sin and consequently when we did not break the law of God. The story of Adam and Eve imagines a time when we were perfect, innocent, whole, connected to God. We enjoyed afternoon walks with the Almighty, frolicking naked in the Garden of Eden.[62] You'd have to call that a pretty cordial relationship! But later in the story we became infected with sin.

---

62. Genesis 2-3.

We fell from grace. We fell into our current sinful condition. And so it came to be that we need to be healed from this sin or suffer eternal death. God tried a variety of strategies to rid humanity of this dread condition. The story of Noah and the flood was an early strategy in the story. God chose a righteous man and his family, kept them safe in an ark, and then wiped the rest of the species from the face of the globe. That didn't work. The very next story concerns people who tried to build a tower tall enough to break through the dome over creation and take over God's domain in the heavens.

Next God chose a people and gave them the law, that is, instructions concerning how to love and be loved in perfect harmony as God intends. This people was to be a blessing to all the families of the earth. The Hebrew scriptures suggest that this remains an ongoing project. The Christian scriptures, while not disagreeing, see the need for something more, something radical. So instead of meting out the punishment upon us, the guilty, God sends his Son to accept that punishment on our behalf. His Son was crucified on our behalf. When Jesus dies, when his blood is shed, (and remember the writers and thinkers of that time thought that blood has magical properties), it's not just Jesus that dies, it's all of the old, fallen, infected humanity that dies along with him.

But that's not the end of the story. Jesus does not stay in the grave; the old humanity dies, to be sure, but a new humanity, one free of sin, rises from the grave. How can this be effective for us? The answer is faith. It is faith that binds us to the destiny of the savior, Jesus the Christ. When we latch hold on to that idea, when we trust that this is what God has done for us, this trust allows us to be healed of our sin and so live in the resurrected, abundant, eternal life of Christ. Because of what God did in Jesus Christ, whether we continue to break God's law or not, the promise is that God looks at us and sees the abundant beauty that lies within us. This is the grace of God. We are no longer identified by the human condition, no longer bound to the inevitable consequences of the human condition. We are free, or to put it more traditionally, we are saved! That's the traditional doctrine of salvation.

This doesn't make a great deal of sense to the modern mind. We don't think blood has magical properties, or that there is a God who needs blood shed as retribution because you had sex before you were married. (It always comes down to sex doesn't it?) But consider, if you think there is a God outside creation, one who is acting upon us, if you think there was a point in history when humankind was perfect, if you think that blood has magical properties and can satisfy God's desire for justice, then this way of formulating the Doctrine of Salvation makes a great deal of sense. It offers a gracious God who takes seriously the consequences of living outside of the integrity of God's love for all. This is a God they knew. It imagines a God that frees us from a hopeless, static existence, bound to our fate and unable to grow or to change. This is a God they knew. It recognizes a God that looks upon them with a love so profound as to not even contemplate separation from them, or they from each other. They knew that God. They knew a God that freed them and allowed them to develop and grow. Is there a way then to understand the Doctrine of Salvation that will make more sense of our worldview while at the same time being faithful to the experiences and insights of those who formulated this doctrine? I think so.

We don't hold to the literal assumptions of the traditional doctrine of salvation, but I think we'd have to agree that the human condition is disturbing. We've gone over this before. We say, "I love you," but we do not mean "I love you, and I will do whatever is in my power to see that your life flourishes." Instead, all too often what we mean by "I love you" is, "You do a good job of filling my current set of needs and don't seem to require anything from me that I can't handle." Let's call that view of love "sin." There is tremendous pain in our world. Just cast your eyes on the unjust economic system we've built. That system is clearly the product of the human condition, "sin." It's the dirty underbelly of the human condition; it's the result of human development to this point, that fight to survive. If you still aren't convinced that there is something seriously wrong, that homo sapiens don't have a long road ahead if we are to reflect the good, the true, and the beautiful, (which I doubt or you wouldn't have read this far), then consider the horrifying spectacle of human cruelty.

The human condition is deeply troubling. If there's no God from the outside who's going to fix it, can we be saved? What would it mean to be saved anyway? Let's try this: it starts with waking up. We wake up to the fact that we are not the sum of our biological drives, that this is not a static world in which we live but a dynamic, evolutionary world. We wake up to the reality that we are not separate, disconnected individuals but rather we are each a unique expression of the seamless fabric of creation itself. Creation moves from one thing to another. It develops and it grows. God's power can be seen in the impulse that drives this process forward. God's power, the Logos of John, lives within us and expresses itself through us. When our eyes are opened to that fact, when we receive it and trust it, when our self-consciousness rises above the bondage of the human condition, when we rend the illusion that we are separate, well then we are saved.

This view offers a gracious God who takes seriously the consequences of living outside of the integrity of God's love for all. This is a God we know. It imagines a God that frees us from a hopeless, static existence, bound to our fate and unable to grow or to change. This is a God we know. It recognizes a God that looks upon us with a love so profound as not even to contemplate separation from us, or we from each other. We know that God, a God who frees us and allows us to develop and grow.

Wake up; you are saved! You are a human being and as such you have what John calls power to become a Child of God, that is, power to be an integral part of the process of evolution in this place. You have the power to change because the creative impulse that has driven creation forward lo these 13.82 billion years, expresses itself within you. The power of sin – bondage to what we think is a static reality—breaks when we wake up to that fact. That is the doctrine of salvation.

In both the traditional and what I might call the evolutionary view of the doctrine of salvation, if we trust, if we wake up to God's way in creation, we are no longer identified by the human condition, no longer bound to the inevitable consequences of the human condition, but instead free to live abundant lives, intimately connected to the presence of God.

That is who we are. To be clear, this is how Christian faith deals with the nature of our being. But the painful truth is that this reality does not express itself in our lives as often as we'd like. And so we come to the doctrine of sanctification. The doctrine of sanctification is how Christian faith works with the issue of becoming. This one is a little easier to think through. In virtually every religious tradition there is this tension between being and becoming. Sanctification is about becoming who we are—Children of God, if you will. We are a unique expression of the love intelligence of the universe, but we must develop so that we more perfectly express that reality. In short we need to grow up. In a traditional Christian faith the Holy Spirit is given to us so that we can become who we are. This is what the Apostle Paul calls "working out our salvation." That kind of language resonates for me. My difficulty comes when I consider that traditionally this working out of our salvation, this work we do to become who we already are, is done under the specter of a wrathful and judging God. Frankly, this is the source of a tremendous portion of the abuse and damage the Christian tradition has done. It is the reason we don't even use the word "sin" in our home. It is too loaded with a God that is anything but loving. Nevertheless it is part and parcel of the traditional Christian doctrines of sanctification and salvation, and if I'm to be faithful to the tradition I need to work through that.

It is true that in this universe there are consequences for actions, though to suggest a one-to-one correspondence stretches credulity beyond the breaking point. The process of evolution moves forward because some element or another is not working in harmony with other elements of creation. It is true that the old is destroyed in favor of the next step in evolution. I can understand how those who did not understand the way nature unfolds might interpret those things as the wrath of God. But surely we do not need to think this way now. In fact to do so flies in the face of a loving God who wants only to make us whole. The First Letter of John says that God literally is this kind of love.[63] We grow up in the presence of a God whose creative power unfolds and expresses itself within and around us. We grow up in love, not in fear, but we do grow up, we do evolve. In fact it is our unique obligation to do so. That is the doctrine of sanctification.

Wake up...grow up—but to what end? This is the issue that the traditional exposition of eschatology seeks to address. Traditionally Christians have spoken about the second coming of Christ—Jesus returns on a white horse, splitting open the heavens re-entering creation and bringing all things to their perfect close. The "new Jerusalem" descends from the heavens, everyone lives in harmony with God and with one another, the whole universe becomes one. I know it sounds fanciful and please, let's be clear, the language of the Revelation of John was never intended to be literal. It was fairytale language from the start, (and pretty cool fairytale language at that).[64] It is a vision of hope, a statement of trust, one we use as we live our lives with that direction in mind.

Do I think it will work that way, Jesus on a white horse? No. But I do believe that creation is moving towards the moment when being and becoming are complete, when all things live in harmony. I emphasize that this is a statement

---

63. First John 4:8.
64. The Revelation of John is actually one of my favorite books of the Bible. I can't resist this little excursus. Once you figure out that it is intended to be metaphorical language you read into it a God whose desire for justice is strong, and whose power is ultimate. You read about the ways of God in the world and those ways are ultimately very bad news for the coercive power structures that believe they rule the world. In the Revelation a beast of the land and a beast of the sea rise up. It is clear from any reading that they refer to the political power of Caesar and its connection to the Emperor's cult, the religious power of the day. Late in the story God tosses them into the lake of burning sulfur to suffer and die forever. That's what God thinks of the marriage of political and religious power.

of faith. It's a conclusion that can't be built on a foundation of verifiable evidence. Oh, there is evidence that says it's not a crazy notion—13.82 billion years from the Big Bang to Shakespeare suggests directionality to me—but that does not constitute proof.

But when we live with that hope, with that directionality and purpose in mind, it means that we have to show up. We're an integral part of that hoped-for future. In that unity where everything comes together in perfect harmony, where the outrageous pain of the world explodes into an outrageous love, you will have to be there. Each of us has a unique perspective, a unique way of living, of loving, and of expressing the being of God. If you don't show up, if you don't play your unique role, if you don't live into your purpose and being, we can't get it done. Creation is incomplete without you living out your purpose, your unique obligation. You are that important.

Wake up. You are a child of God; you are not bound and limited by a static human condition. The power that drives our evolving universe is expressing itself through you. Grow up. Let that reality take hold so that you evolve and are transformed by the creative love of God. Show up. You are an expression of that love. If you do not play your unique role in this evolving project called life, we cannot come together in perfect harmony. You are an integral part of the beauty that opens our hearts and makes us whole. It's time for us all to wake up to that reality.

Chapter 12

Meet Me in Galilee

When the Sabbath was over, [that is to say when the time out of time was over], Mary Magdalene and Mary the mother of James and Salome bought spices so that they might go and anoint Jesus. Very early on the first day of the week when the sun had risen, they went to the tomb. They had been saying to one another who would roll away the stone for us from the entrance to the tomb. When they looked up, they saw that the stone which was very large had already been rolled back. As they entered the tomb, they saw a young man dressed in a white robe sitting on the right side. They were alarmed. The young man said to them, do not be alarmed. You are looking for Jesus of Nazareth who was crucified. He has been raised. He is not here. Look, there's the place where they laid him. Go now, tell his disciples, tell Peter, that he is going ahead of you to Galilee. There you will see him exactly as he told you. So, the women went out, fled from the tomb, for terror and amazement had seized them. They said nothing to anyone, for they were afraid.

Mark 16:1-8

The dance of creation is an extraordinary thing, don't you think? From the far reaches of the cosmos, to the tiniest little microbes, this dance plays out. You know, the year my father was born we didn't know there was more than one galaxy. It was only in 1917 that we figured out that Andromeda, that little fuzzy spot, was actually a whole other galaxy. Think of how much we have learned about this incredible, extraordinary, beautiful creation since then.

You know there are whole worlds and creatures that go on about their lives, go on their journeys, without us having any conscious awareness of them at all. It's an extraordinary and beautiful world.

Yet for all that beauty, the process of life and death, the process that makes up this creation, makes this creation somewhat dangerous and even brutal.

Consider the length and breadth of human travail, the sorrow that we feel, the number of things going on in the world that simply don't live up to the unity and hope and gorgeousness of creation. Millions of people do not have enough food to eat, and it's not because there isn't enough food to go round. It's because human society has failed to find ways to distribute that food. It's because human society has failed to find ways for every human being to work productively in such a way that they can provide for their needs. Or consider the clash of worldviews on this earth. The world's become small at a time when there isn't a world big enough for radical Islam and fundamentalist Christianity to co-exist without erupting into anger and violence.

There's not much we can do about that. The internet has made the space between us so small. Everybody hears what everybody else says. Somebody wrote a comment on my blog a while ago. Whoever it was, he was pretty angry about what I'd written and he said something about my being a heretic, I ought not to call myself a Christian, and so on. Okay, that's the way that is. But all I could think was that I wish he hadn't read my post. I even wrote that up in the next couple of posts. "If you don't like what I'm saying, then stop reading. I'm not writing this to make you angry." Ours was a clash of worldviews.

I think of Pope Francis. What an incredibly difficult job he has. He's supposed to be leading a church in which some adherents believe in magic and some don't really believe there's any God but they opt to go through the religious motions anyway. His is an enormously difficult task at a time when starvation of the human spirit is endemic to our society.

But let's not focus only on the difficult, on human finitude, for there are moments of redemption, right? There are those moments when someone can come back from horrible injury inflicted by the desperate violence of guns and find the embrace of colleagues, the joy that people feel when you get well again. It's just that in a real world those moments of joy don't always happen. These are what I call cross moments, moments of destruction in creation.

This anxiety and fear is what it's like for us in the world right at the edge, always at the edge of creation's next step. But that's also precisely where evolution happens, always at the edge —the edge of life and death, the edge of our emotions, the edge of our oceans — that's where it takes place.

Evolution responds to stress and chaos as it unfolds, each moment transcending and including the moment that came before it, each step more complex, more unified than before, always moving towards Shalom, towards wholeness, towards a just peace where each person plays her unique and vital role. This evolving creation cannot be complete without you. God can't get it done without you.

Everything evolves. Internally and externally, individually and as a group, everything evolves. The structure of human economies evolve, and those structures affect the evolution of internal cultural values, which in turn affects the way individuals develop morally and spiritually, which in turn affects how we develop physically. Around and around it goes; step by step, always at that moment of chaos we await that creative Word, that creative moment from God. And that moment brings something surprising into being: new life, a life we can't conceive of when we're in the midst of chaos.

We all have those moments, and when they come we often confront a moment of choice. In that chaotic moment we can repeat the deadly cycle that's brought us to this moment of history, or we can move ahead and let the new emerge.

My son Matthew was home from college recently. We're very proud of him. One of the things we're proud of is that he earned his black belt in Kenpo Karate. Each time he went through a belt test he took another step forward. There was always a ceremony, a time to celebrate what had happened. He'd kneel with his eyes closed; his Sensei would ask him to remember or reflect upon everything that had gone on since the last belt test—all the things he'd learned, all the disappointments he'd felt, all that sense of accomplishment when he learned a new form, a new move. As he did that, his Sensei placed his new belt in front of him. Then, at the right moment, when he was ready, he took off his old belt, put it behind him, and put on the new one as a sign of his evolution, his next step.

That's the way it is. Evolution steps forward, human beings step forward. That is exactly what the story of the cross and the resurrection is about. Not only are evolution and faith not at odds, they are two sides of the same coin. When Christ died, the old passed away. When Christ was raised, something fresh and new emerged out of the chaos of death. The old is left behind and the new comes forth. That's the good news, you know. The good news of the gospel is that no matter how low you feel you've gone, no matter your flaw, no matter what burden you carry, no matter what the dream left unfulfilled, there is a next. There is a next because the Spirit of God that hovers right above that emptiness drives creation forward.

When the women came to the tomb that day, they had to be wondering what was next. They had to be wondering how they were going to get past this crisis, this horror. Their dear friend and teacher, the one that had given them solidity and identity, had been crucified, and was dead and buried. They didn't know whether anything could emerge from this moment so they came mourning.

The interesting thing is that the Gospel of Mark, the whole thing, was written to tell anyone who will listen how to go about growing into that next step, how to go about evolving into that new resurrection moment instead of remaining stuck in the cycle that brought us to this place. It's what the book of Mark is about.

It begins with Jesus being baptized; the Spirit of God fills Jesus the Christ and drives him into the wilderness to be spiritually formed. That formation continued throughout his life. There was a cadence in the Gospel of Mark, a cadence between Jesus moving out into the world and moving back into the emptiness where his Spirit could be renewed.

Spiritual formation is key to growing up and growing through chaos into new hope. There is any number of ways to do it. Some people meditate every day. I have a pastor friend who carries seven smooth stones in her left pocket. Whenever she feels one, she stops and thinks to say a quick prayer of thanks, then transfers it into the right pocket. It's her goal to make sure all seven stones make it into the right pocket by the end of the day.

There are many things that you can do to stop, remove the fake pleasure that fills our world, and instead be in that place where the Spirit in you can be recognized and nourished. Perhaps you love to study and read about science. Study is one of the classic spiritual disciplines. It's been part of our faith tradition from the start. But study is more than just learning. At the end of learning comes a moment's reflection about the power of God that makes creation unfold, about the power that nourishes the Spirit within.

The Gospel of Mark shows us a Jesus who wrestled with a living tradition. He wrestled with the Jewish traditions, the Jewish God, and was trying to describe this God to an entirely different society than had known it before. He'd faced the Greco-Roman world, as did the disciples following him, and looked for a way to talk about the same God, using different words, words that would communicate to them.

Isn't that what we need today—to talk about the same God, but to find ways to talk about that God that make sense to the world around us today. I'm convinced that the reason the church is failing is because we have not found those words. We're looking for words that are as different from classic Christianity as Christianity was from Ancient Judaism; we're looking for words that are every bit the same as Christianity was to Ancient Judaism. But though they may be new words, they're about the same God, one God, gracious, unfolding, loving.

Mark's Gospel depicts Jesus as serving the people on the edges of society and seeking to change the systems and structures that create injustice in the world. That is what got him in trouble. He went in and cleared out the money changers in the temple because he was interested in changing the entrenched structures of that society, so that both the poor and the rich could be met by the strength and the power of God.

Mark shows us a Jesus who formed a group of people that could work together, each playing a unique and vital role. The reign of God can only become a reality when all are woven together in unity.

The whole Gospel of Mark is there is to tell us how Jesus moved from Galilee, all the way to Jerusalem, through the chaos of the cross, and through to that moment of resurrection. What did he have to say to the women? What message did he leave at this moment when they longed to find their way through to what is next?

"Meet me in Galilee when you're ready," he said. Meet me in Galilee. If you do, the Spirit of God will drive you into the wilderness and your spiritual formation will begin. Meet me in Galilee. You and I can wrestle with a living tradition that points towards the God of love; you and I can find the words that communicate clearly in this time and this place. Meet me in Galilee, he said, and we will serve those at the edges of society. Meet me in Galilee, where you and all the others reading these words can be woven together into a perfect whole. Spirit can't get it done without you. Meet me in Galilee—but be prepared, because it is in Galilee, on the edge of chaos, hovering in emptiness, that I will ask you to take up your cross and follow me.

But know this: when you take up that cross, when you are willing to take that step into the chaos and trust God's power to bring about the next moment of growth, you will see beauty emerge. The new life will surprise you and Easter morning will finally make sense. When you're ready, put on your next belt, and meet me in Galilee.

PART IV
APPENDICES

Two Spiritual Exercises You Might Have Missed

If what we're trying to do is become the unique expression of the creative love dynamic that animates creation, which is what I think gives life meaning and purpose, then we need to remain deeply grounded in that love. How? Many, many people meditate. That is a wonderful and holy way to remain open to the presence, but I've always struggled with meditation. I still do it because I think that meditating is part of a full connection to God, but there are other practices that have a greater impact on me. I offer them to you here.

Writing Love Letters

That's right, writing love letters is a spiritual practice. There is even a nascent love letter writing movement. Go to outragesouloveletters.com to join if you're so inspired. These love letters can be to anyone. They can be to people you know or people you don't. I wanted a challenge one evening and so I wrote one to Robert Mueller, retired Director of the FBI, one evening after I heard him speak. You can even write letters to yourself. In fact I think that's a great idea, and of course, you can write them to God, or the Source, or the ground of being, however you conceive of all that it is. It almost doesn't matter though to whom you write; it is the practice of writing love letters that opens the heart and lets love flow. If you get in a space to write a love letter every day for 90 days, a great way to begin, it changes you. That's all I can say; it just changes you.

I wrote 30 or so love letters recently; I put them online which may not have been a good idea; it did sort of cramp my

style. http://www.patheos.com/blogs/christianityforthesbnr/
After I'd written those initial letters though, I took a break. They were hard to write and I was traveling. But more than that I found that I was looking for something deeper in the practice. I posted the following reflection as part of my effort to search that out. I offer it here in the hopes it may stimulate your imagination and get you to consider putting more love into the world.

> You may or may not have noticed that I've taken a short break from writing these love letters. It has proved to be both a challenging and a beautiful practice. Finding that space within myself that seeks what is beautiful and expressing love and gratitude for it every day is easier said than done. Sometimes the pressures of life itself, those daily pressures that keep us distracted, make it hard. But it is amazing how making an effort to open yourself to love every day brings up those deeper fractures, the life trajectory pains and traumas. These two conspire to make it hard to find that heart space you need to find if you're to write the kind of love letter I want to write. That is, of course, the point of the practice, and so I get it, I must pick up my pen again and open to that space every day, whether I feel inspired or not.
>
> But there is something else going on here in the midst of this love letter practice. It's been showing itself more and more these last couple of weeks and it feels important. Maybe it's happened as a result of the writing I've done thus far, maybe it's because I feel Spirit calling me to crack open, or is it break down, and surrender my desires, my hopes, my dreams, altruistic

though they may be, and sit in the presence of the One whose love defines us all.

I guess I'm saying that I'm pretty good at imagining what love is supposed to be – some of these letters are pretty damn good at it. But no, there is something more that I'm after. The love that I've been offering here is a kind of appreciative love. We could call it eros – that is, I see something and want to enjoy the value in it, then I express gratitude for the gorgeous gift I've received. There are people in this world I love so much it can bring me to tears. All that is fine, great even; nothing wrong with that. That yearning could be described as the evolutionary impulse that drives all there is. But there is a greater dance of love still than that. I've written before but not felt before, (at least not in this way), the importance of agape in the dance of love. Agape differs from eros as it sees an object and wants to put value into it. It is a creative love. Marc, who I've mentioned often in this book mostly because the book itself is a reflection on his teaching, says that this love is the "love before creation," the love that generated the big bang. Marc doesn't usually distinguish between eros and agape in his work; I do. (I don't think we really disagree; I'm just emphasizing a dance between the two partner loves where Marc seems to use eros to describe the dance itself.) Neither love by itself will get us much of anywhere; it's the dance that does it. For the yearning we feel is essential to drive us forward. But that creative word, that love that begins before desire, before creation, that impulse to love without return, but just love in order to love, is something I aspire to. It is. I've come to understand the Outrageous Love we seek.

The letters I've written to date are letters with eros at their heart. They have expressed that gratitude and love I feel when I consider the beauty and complexity of God's incredible creation as it is expressed in the people I know – or sometimes that I don't know. But I'm after more than that now. I want to express that love before creation, simply that impulse to love for love. I'll keep writing now. Some of the letters will undoubtedly reflect an erotic love, that is, that part of the dance of love that is about yearning and enjoyment. That is likely to be so precisely because it is a dance. But my aim is to find that space within that simply loves – the love before creation, before gratitude, the love that fills us with eros and lets the dance begin.

The practice is transformative. I invite you to open up and try. We could use a lot more love in the world!

Confession

I know: confession isn't the most popular of spiritual practices. The absurdity and abuse of the practice gives it a bad name, but it has been THE central spiritual practice of the Christian religion for hundreds and hundreds of years. Confession builds communities of forgiveness. It lets us take what is not conscious to us in our life, what is subject as I've said elsewhere in the book, and make it conscious, make it an object, a pattern of behavior that can be changed. I wrote the following reflection on confession at a time when our congregation was at least considering making it more a part of our worship. We abandoned the practice though; it was a bit too intense. But that's why I recommend it to you.

The letter of James, the entire letter, is about building a community of forgiveness. A community that enables one another to grow and to become whole. Many of us—I'll say it for myself—will say, "I'm a good person," but a whole person? A complete person? A fulfilled person? I can't make that claim. Nor could the people that received James' letter. So James was saying "We want a community that helps one another to grow toward that wonder of being in the midst of God's love so it can be shared." Back in that day they used to think that if you got physically sick it meant there was some interruption of the flow of God's creative grace. If you are sick then something is wrong between you and God. Actually, we think that a lot today too about several things. There is an interruption in the flow of grace that makes us not well, not whole, not complete, not joyful. What's his advice? Confess your sins to one another so that you may be healed. Confess your sins to one another, confess the blockage that you find in God's grace, so that you may be healed and become more healed and more whole, filled with joy. Confess your sins to one another.

Maybe they're on to something. It's possible that good liberal Presbyterians who don't talk about an angry god, might have run a little bit far and a little bit fast from the traditions that pay attention to what God thinks we should do and not do. It has become quite common not to confess sin in worship services across the country like we did when I was a kid. Confession is such a downer. We don't pay a whole lot of attention to confessing because it takes some time to understand where the flow of God's grace is blocked. It occurs to me that it is a little painful to pay attention to the pain and the shame that runs deep within us. It's difficult and painful for us to recognize what the blockage is in God's grace. I understand why we avoid confession; but I wonder if we are not missing opportunities for growth. Maybe the Roman Catholics of my youth were on to something.

I'm thinking we need to re-establish the confessional—*not* to a Priest mind you, though it might be that some individuals would want to do it that way. But it occurs to me that we need to have an opportunity to move towards transformation and growth and that happens as we confess what has been called sin—a separation from the presence of God - to one another so that we may be healed. What would that look like? What would it look like to confess our sins to one another?

I think the first thing you would need is a confessor. Somebody to confess to and that can't be just anyone. It needs to be someone who understands the depth of their own rebellion to God; the depth of their own difficulties and struggles in becoming whole. Because if you understand your own rebellion, your own false self, then you don't listen with judgment to others. You don't do the comparison thing. Instead you are able to listen to another person who is struggling as they seek to grow and become whole, recognizing that we are all in this together. You need a confessor who isn't going to judge.

You need one who can help you work out the kind of steps you might take in order to become whole. That's what all the 'Our Fathers' and 'Hail Mary's' were about you know. I always thought the way it worked was that you had to say a certain number of 'Our Fathers' and a certain number of 'Hail Marys' after you confessed your sin so you could work off the black marks. But that wasn't the point at all. The point was supposed to be that while you say those prayers you are opening up enough space in your soul for grace to come in and heal. It was intended to be a healing exercise. You are going to need somebody to help you figure out what the healing exercises might be. What are the steps we need to take in order to be transformed and whole?

Luther said he was sure that he could confess his sins to God all by himself but he wouldn't be able to hear forgiveness unless he heard it from another human voice. We need someone who can communicate the love of God at that moment. At that moment of extreme vulnerability. Then maybe we have a chance of sitting down with our lives and asking ourselves some deep questions about the blockages to the flow of grace in our life, or the things that keep us from loving one another and keep us from communing with holy God. That's not the sort of thing you do in 10 seconds on Sunday morning.

I have a friend who remained in the Catholic Church and all through college she went to church every day. She went to Mass every day. She took confession very seriously; about once every year or two, she would sit down and say "This is a real moment of growth for me." She would go through her life very carefully. She would go see her priest and confess those things and talk about those steps she might take to grow forward. She referred to those as seminal confessions. The beginning ones. Any other confessions she did referred back to it. This is what a confessional might look like.

We confess our sins; we do penance NOT with an eye towards appeasing an angry god, but an eye toward the possibility of growing and becoming whole that our joy may be complete. God is love. God seeks nothing but your complete health and wholeness. So I invite you to consider confessing your sins to one another that you may be healed.

Death of the Church[65]

When it was noon darkness came over the whole land until it was three in the afternoon. At three o'clock Jesus cried out in a loud voice, "Eloi, Eloi, lema sabbachthani," which means, "My God, my God, why have you forsaken me?" When some of the bystanders heard it, they said, "Listen he is calling for Elijah." Someone ran, filled a sponge with sour wine, put it on a stick, and gave it to him to drink, saying, 'Let's see whether Elijah will come to take him down' Then Jesus gave a loud cry, and breathed his last.

Mark 15:33-37

I'd like us to consider this text and the death of the Church in the context of evolution and Christian faith. By evolution I specifically do not mean a discussion of a six-day creation, with God resting on the seventh. I really, really hope that argument's over and done with. No, I mean evolution as the way in which everything unfolds in all of creation. Everything evolves. It's the creative process, driven by the Spirit of God, that is unfolding, I believe towards that longed for telos, the time of shalom and peace in the presence of God, that the Scriptures describe.

Evolution happens right at the edge of things. That's how it works. In the midst of the chaos when a system ceases

---

65. This sermon is very similar to "Meet Me in Galilee" but specifically addresses the undeniable reality of a dying mainline church.

to function, there is a new step forward in the evolution of creation. Take the first ecological crisis on earth, for instance. Early in the evolution of life there were colonies of bacteria that lived on the boundary between the oceans and the land. Some bacteria had evolved to perform a simple photosynthetic process; they were able to take light energy and turn it into chemical energy, which they could use to flourish. The by-product of that photosynthesis was oxygen. Things went well for these bacteria until enough of them produced enough oxygen that it polluted their atmosphere. I say polluted because these bacteria could not live in an oxygen-rich atmosphere. They were poisoning their own environment. Sound familiar?

As the biological system came under this stress, as resources became scarce, bacterial colonies in effect attacked other colonies in search of a food source. One might have expected that over time an equilibrium would develop where just the right number of bacteria were in harmonic balance with just the right amount of oxygen being produced, but instead something novel, unpredictable, and surprising happened. That's how evolution happens: new and creative moves of evolution emerge from the chaos and stress of a system as it breaks down. In this case, as bacterial colonies "collided" with one another seeking food at the edge of the sea, some cells came together in such a way that they became the first eukaryote cells, the first animal cells. In contrast to bacterial cells, animal cells are able to use oxygen, and they thrived in the "polluted" atmosphere. And so creation on our planet evolved in such a way that balanced plant cells that produce oxygen with animal cells that use oxygen.

It was a surprising move forward. That's how evolution works. Right at the moment of stress, right when the old creation is dying and breaking down, a new creation emerges.

There are three characteristics to any such evolutionary move: First, an old form of creation is transcended. In our example, the original bacteria are transcended. But its constituent parts are included into the next iteration of creation. So characteristic one of evolution is: transcend and include.

Second, each step produces more complexity. The new system of plant and animal cells is certainly more complex than the original bacterial communities. So characteristic two of evolution is: increasing complexity. Finally, each step is a surprise, it is novel, like when two hydrogen atoms and an oxygen atom came together. You could probably have figured out from their valances that those molecules might stick together, but if you'd never seen it before, you never would have predicted the property of flow. So characteristic three of evolution is: novelty. Step by step in the midst of chaos, right at the edge of things, this is how evolution moves forward.

What is really interesting to me is that this evolutionary process is exactly what happens in the cross and the resurrection.

When Jesus dies on the edge of society and then rises, an old life form of life is transcended and yet included in what is next. There was some coherence between the Jesus who his disciples knew and the resurrected Jesus – coherence, but they weren't the same either. Next, the resurrection was a novel moment in creation.[66] Jesus rose as a new creation, a new human being, and that new human being is infinitely more complex and unified with all that is than the Jesus the disciples had known. To what degree this is a metaphor and to what degree an ontological reality is a subject for another time, but either way, the motif of cross and resurrection, the very center of our faith, points right at the process of evolution. Not only are cross and resurrection not in conflict with evolution, they are two sides of the very same coin. It is through the process of death and new life that the process of creation, the evolution of all that is, unfolds towards unity and shalom.

This unfolding process happens in all facets of creation – individually and in groups, internally and externally. Our bodies evolve, yes, but the internal landscape of our life does

---

66. This could be argued, I know, on historical grounds. There are reports of resurrections in other cultures, but in the world of the story of Jesus, this was novelty.

as well. Researchers have shown, for instance, that individual human beings evolve morally from an egocentric sense of the self, where we care only for ourselves, to an ethnocentric sense of the self, where we identify with a group, to a world-centric sense of self, where we see ourselves connected to all people, to a kosmo-centric sense of self, where we identify with all that is and recognize our small but unique role in the unified whole.

The structures of society evolve as well. Researchers have traced economic and technological evolution. Human society was one time organized around the technologies of the hunter and gatherer. Then we evolved into agricultural communities. Then we became an industrial society. Each step of the way we were transcending and including what went before, always moving toward greater complexity, always surprised by the unpredictable next.

This same evolutionary process of transcending and including takes place within the inner, religious, and cultural values of human society. Our worldviews have evolved. They began with a magical orientation to creation, in which spirits of all kinds control what is happening and we offer gifts of coconuts and pineapples to volcanoes and such to appease them. This was a typical orientation for tribal societies, but as tribes banded into nations, they needed something other than blood to hold them together, and so came the birth of the mythic worldview. Stories are told that bring coherence and purpose to human society. In our tradition, twelve tribes came together and saw themselves as carrying the blessing of God for all people. Of course at a certain point those myths break down. They are deconstructed in a modernist worldview and our cultural values shift. We seek truth through by experimentation, that is, until the postmodernist comes along and says, "Truth? You've got to be kidding me. There is no such thing because all truth is perspectival."

Each time, a moment of chaos yields new creation, new forms of complexity, and unity. On Good Friday in the church we focus on the reality that this is a terrifying, painful process because there's always cross before there's resurrection. There's always death of the old before emergence of the new. One way to look at the death and resurrection of Jesus in the Gospel of Luke is to see a shift in cultural history, a moment when the old was passing and the new was emerging. When Jesus died upon that cross, the old passed away and the disciples waited for the new to emerge. The body of Christ was on the cross at the moment when Judaism met the Greco-Roman world and Jesus' disciples were awaiting the next.

The body of Christ is on the cross again today. Every time the mythic church meets modernism, it loses the framework that gives it life and it begins to shrink and die. It's the way things unfold in an evolving creation. It's unsettling, terrifying if we really think about it, but we really are awaiting whatever is next. So my question for us, a question answered by this text from Mark, is this: As we look at the cross on this day, how can we be faithful to the God who drives creation forward? How can we live our lives, mindful of our own unique obligation to perform the acts of love only we can perform in service of Spirit's next move in creation?

The Gospel speaks loud and clear. In fact, it's the reason the Gospel of Mark was written: to help us understand how to be faithful at the moment of death, at the moment we wait for new creation to emerge. Jesus made it clear to the women when they came Easter morning: Go tell the disciples to meet me in Galilee, *meet me on the edge of the sea, right at the boundary of chaos where something new can emerge.*

"Meet me in Galilee when you're ready," he was saying, "and Spirit will drive you into the wilderness so that your spiritual formation may begin. Meet me in Galilee and we – you reading these words, and me — will find ways to re-describe a living truth to a very different culture. We'll find a way to describe a faith that is as different from Christianity as Christianity was from Ancient Judaism. We will find a way to describe a faith that is as much the same as Christianity as Christianity was to Ancient Judaism. Meet me in Galilee and we will serve people on the edges of society, we will open our hearts, be welcomed and welcome them into the unified whole. Meet me in Galilee and you and I and many others will join together. We will show the world an alternative to the fractured, lonely, suffering society with its fake pleasures and hollow dreams. We will be woven together into the new body of Christ, a new whole.

Meet me in Galilee, but be prepared: be prepared for chaos to overwhelm and for something unpredictable to take place. Meet me in Galilee, but be prepared, because it's there that I will ask you to take up your cross and follow me."

Continuing the Conversation

This book is intended to start a conversation not finish it. You should feel free to log onto either of my blogs, http://www.patheos.com/blogs/christianityforthesbnr/ or http://www.gracecomesfirst.net, join the conversation, and explore whatever resources you might find. http://www.patheos.com, the largest inter-religious site on the web provides both resources and community to those who are seeking. I'm delighted to write for the site.

You can find out more about my wife's coaching process using unique self dharma from an evolutionary worldview at http://www.barbaraalexander.net or www.uniqueselfcoaching.com. This form of coaching is primarily for people who have tried and tried again to make a breakthrough of some kind in their life and haven't been able to bring it to fruition . . . and it works! I don't know why I should be surprised, the theoretical foundations are solid, but to watch people developing when they engage it has been thrilling indeed. I do not mean to suggest that it is some sort of easy, three-step process to spiritual fulfillment. No, it is hard and sometimes painful work, (like any real effort at growth), but when it is engaged, wonderful things happen.

I too offer Unique Self Coaching along with broader spiritual and theological counsel should someone be interested in exploring ideas about Christian faith one on one. The first conversation is always free and sometimes one conversation is all that is needed, so contact me at sam@gracecomesfirst.net. From there we can figure out together what would be best.

As I preached the sermon series, I read Carter Phipps' book, *Evolutionaries Unlocking the Spiritual and Cultural Potential of Science's Greatest Idea*. It absolutely lit me up. Carter traces the development of evolutionary thought in an engaging and inspiring way. For a broader grounding in how the theory of evolution applies to all of creation, read Carter Phipps. http://www.carterphipps.com/ Though he engages important and complex ideas, he is easy to understand.

Dr. Marc Gafni has been a true friend and conversation partner. When he opens up Torah I swear it lights up with the presence of God. He founded the Center for Integral Wisdom of which I'm a part. Exploring his ideas can be exhilarating.

Finally, I'd like to thank my seminary theology professor, Douglas Ottati, who, when I was at my most obnoxious, provided the perspective I would eventually need to grow up in faith. Doug, how did you stand it?

UNIQUE SELF
COACHING COLLECTIVE

Afterword by Barbara Alexander

I'm honored to write the afterword for my husband's book for many reasons but the most important is that I have the most intimate view of his evolution, intellectually and experientially. When I met Sam sixteen years ago he was spiritually in the mythic level of development. Three events took place in the space of two years that shattered his carefully constructed faith structure. First, his wife died after a ten-year battle with cancer. Next, he went to Princeton Seminary for a sabbatical year of study. Last, I moved to the East Coast and began seminary studies at Union Seminary in New York.

The first two events would have been enough to move Sam to deconstruct his faith structure, but it's no overstatement to say that I pushed him right over the edge! I didn't mean to really, I was simply in a different place theologically and challenged him to delve deeply into what gave him meaning and purpose. It was a good thing that we had a solid friendship that grew over the years into a deep love. We needed both the deep care and respect for each other to find our way forward from such different points of view. But find our way we did and we continue our journey of growth and change together.

Sam likes to say that he preaches with me on one shoulder. Often I am asking this question, "How?" Being a psychological clinician and a spiritual practitioner, I am always looking for the how. How do we change and grow? How do we establish new patterns of behavior? How do we experience oneness with Ultimate Reality? For that reason, I am critical of those who wax eloquent about what we should believe and how we should act if they do not also provide a road map entitled, How. For while great oratory can indeed be a transmission that impacts one deeply, and even creates openings for change, I believe that truly inspired words of wisdom include a way forward— the how.

Wake Up! Grow Up! Show Up! That's the wisdom of the Marc Gafni's Unique Self Teaching, which my husband has done a brilliant job of putting into a Christian context. It's been all about developing relationships, cultivating creativity and spiritual depth so that we can do work in the world that has meaning and purpose. Wake up to what is real; you are not a skin-encapsulated ego. You are not a separate self. Rather you are a unique expression of the One, the love intelligence that animates the universe. Grow up, raise your consciousness and learn to recognize what's valuable and what must be left behind within each level of development so that you expand your circles of care. Show up, for it is only when you live your unique gift, when you perform those acts of love you were born to perform, things no one else can do, that our society will evolve beyond this polarized, consumptive, self-destructive moment. It is only when we live the unique obligation offered us by the power driving evolution forward that the dawn will rise on a new creation. "YES," you might say, . . . "but how?" How do I Wake Up, Grow Up and Show Up?

The answer is practice. We believe that everyone has a

unique purpose and that joy arises naturally when one lives into the reality of their unique calling as a gift to the world. This is what it means to be living as a Unique Self. The latest research in human development confirms what empirical wisdom and spiritual teachings worldwide have always affirmed: human consciousness is an evolutionary process that continues to develop throughout life. Look around you and it's clear this does not happen naturally to all of humanity. In order to develop beyond the culture's "center of gravity" it takes commitment and practice.

So here is what I would like you to do. If this book has moved you toward further growth, find methods that enable you to look at your life and make changes. That is how change happens. The reality is that each of us holds onto False Core Beliefs, beliefs that emerged from the incorrect assumption that you are a separate self, living in isolation, a "skin-encapsulated ego." Learn how to let go of your False Core Beliefs so that you can drop deeply into connection with the One. Discover how to open your heart to yourself and others in a way that encompasses a circle much larger than you ever imagined. Feel the creative impulse of evolution alive in you as you offer your gifts to the world.

The process my colleague, Claire Molinard, and I developed, Unique Self Coaching www.uniqueselfcoaching.com, is one of those methodologies. It is grounded in the Unique Self Teaching and is a powerful change technology. It has been stunning to watch it work in the lives of those who engage the practices. This work is why I get up every day. When people engage the practices in the process, they take significant steps toward living into their Unique Self. That said, there are many other powerful methodologies available in the world. Never before have we had so many paths available to us. Use them! Practice, and open to the irreducible expression of Divine love that you are. The world really needs you to do that; you will find that a life lived in this way offers deep satisfaction.

Unique Self Certification Program Founders

Barbara Alexander is an Integral Master Coach and teacher. Her passion for human development spans 35 years of training and practice in integral coaching, integral theory, counseling psychology and Spiritual Direction. She is a long time practitioner in the Theravada Buddhist and contemplative Christian traditions.

barbara@barbaraalexander.com

Claire Molinard is an Integral Master Coach and teacher. She works in private practice and as faculty for integral coaching Canada (ICC). Her spiritual practice spans over 20 years exploring various traditions Eastern and Western.

clairemolinard@gmail.com